101

WAYS TO WIN
AT GOLF

By Dick Aultman and the
editors of GOLF DIGEST

Illustrated by Elmer Wexler

A Golf Digest Book

Published by Golf Digest/Tennis Inc.,
A New York Times Company,
495 Westport Avenue,
Norwalk, Connecticut 06856

Trade book distribution by
Simon and Schuster,
A Division of Gulf & Western Corporation,
New York, New York 10020

First Printing
ISBN: 0-914178-40-7
Library of Congress: 80-66689
Manufactured in the United
States of America

Cover and book design by Dorothy Geiser.
Typesetting by Intercontinental Publica-
tions, Westport, Conn.
Printing and binding by R.R. Donnelley &
Sons.

Table of Contents

I.
Setup
and Swing

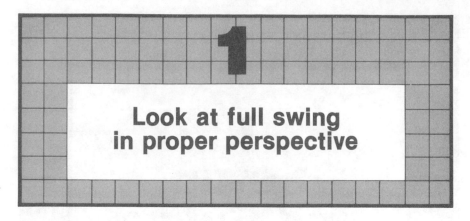

Look at full swing in proper perspective

You may be surprised to know that the typical golfer's clubhead travels at least 40 feet during the course of a full swing with a driver!

Of this total, the club is in contact with the ball for only an inch or two. Obviously, what you do in the rest of the 40-foot swing ultimately determines what happens in the couple of inches at impact—and that's a lot of footage to conquer.

You will be more likely to make solid contact and hit good shots if you keep this perspective of the swing in mind. Don't get bogged down in details.

Efforts to make a pretty swing are wasted—are even detrimental—if your involvement in details makes you forget the main goal of solid contact.

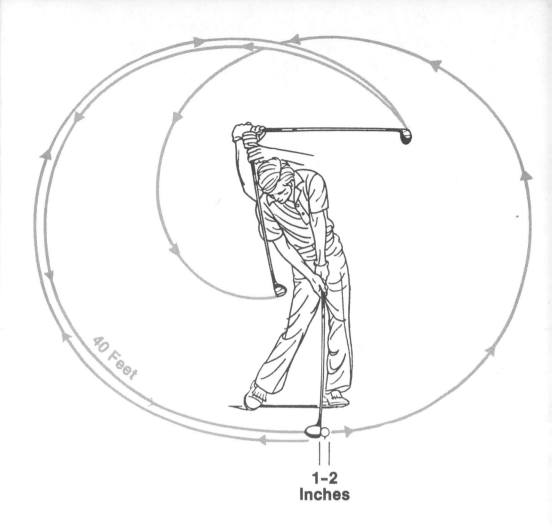

40 Feet

1-2
Inches

Grip lightly
for more length

What makes a golf ball travel a long way?

The most common answer to this question is "clubhead speed." It is a good answer, but incomplete.

A better answer would be "clubhead speed *squarely applied to the ball.*"

The distinction is vital because so many golfers, in striving for ultimate clubhead speed, create too much tension, primarily in their hands and fingers. Extreme grip tension not only stifles clubhead speed, it also inhibits a free and natural squaring of the clubface to the ball.

You should hold the club lightly, both before and *throughout* your swing. This probably will take some conscious effort at first; all instincts tell us that we need a tight grip to give the ball a sound smack.

There probably is no better guide to proper grip pressure than that suggested by Sam Snead, golf's all-time leading tournament winner.

"Hold the club as you would a small bird," says Sam, "with no more pressure than needed to keep it from flying away."

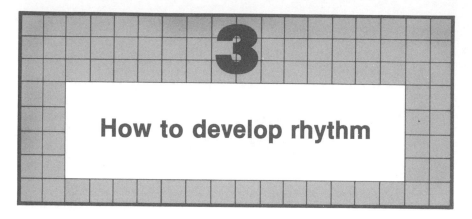

How to develop rhythm

There have been great golfers with fast backswings, such as Arnold Palmer, and there have been great golfers with relatively slow backswings, such as Gene Littler.

But they all share one common denominator. They have learned to let the club complete its backswing before they swing back down toward the ball.

The result is a definite rhythm or beat to their swings, a separation between backswing and forward swing on all shots, from 300-yard drives to three-foot putts.

The place for you to develop this kind of rhythm initially is on three-foot putts. Practice these putts with only your left hand on the club.

You will find it difficult to control the club until you be-

gin to swing your arm rhythmically, finishing your backstroke before you begin your forward stroke.

Once you feel the beat, move on to longer putts, still with only the left hand holding the club. Again, feel the beat, the separation between backstroke and forward stroke. Then do the same on short shots from off the green with a lofted iron.

Finally, once you can make solid contact consistently, move on to full shots, first with a short iron and both hands on the club. Retain the same rhythm that you were forced to employ with only one hand and arm controlling your swing. Gradually build up to the longer clubs, and when your rhythm goes awry revert to the one-handed putting drill and work your way up again.

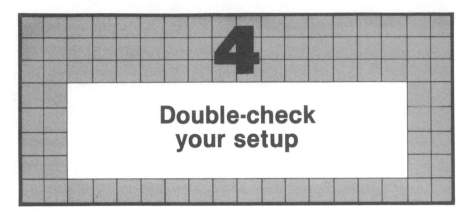

Double-check your setup

Good golf is largely a matter of consistency. Most players know that bad shots stem from bad swings, so they change their swings after making bad shots. This continual changing of swing pattern leads to inconsistency.

What you should realize is that most bad swings result from an incorrect preswing position. The root cause of most bad shots lies in the way a player aims the club and/or positions his body in relation to the ball and his target line.

Rather than change your swing to prevent bad shots, first set two clubs on the ground as shown here—one running parallel to your target line, the other at right angles to it from the ball.

Use the outer club as a guide for aiming your clubface to the target. The face should be set square to the outer clubshaft. Also use this club as a guide for your alignment. Set your entire body, from toes to shoulders, parallel with it.

Use the other club to show you where you are playing the ball in relation to your feet. On normal full shots this club should extend just inside your left heel.

We all slip into patterns of misaiming and misaligning from time to time, and sooner or later they lead to bad swinging. So use this two-club checkout drill at the start of each practice session.

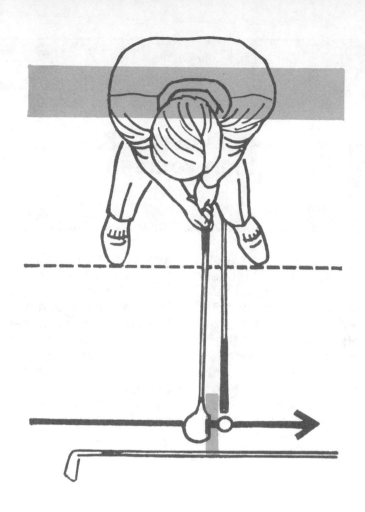

Aim your club, then yourself

Many golfers set their feet before they set the clubhead behind the ball. Since the stance more or less ordains where the club will be aimed, any mispositioning of the feet originally will create a misaimed clubface.

Good golfers always position the club behind the ball first, taking care that it is aimed down their intended flight path. Then they conclude the positioning of their feet and the alignment of their hips and shoulders. They also take care not to alter the aim of the club as they adjust their feet and bodies.

Aim your club first, then your feet and body.

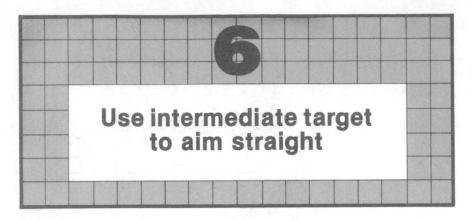

6

Use intermediate target to aim straight

Most golfers unknowingly but consistently misaim the clubface as they prepare to swing.

Misaiming, in time, will instinctively cause a player to adjust his or her swing to try to make the ball finish on target. Usually the adjustment will rob the player of clubhead speed and solid contact.

To check your aiming:

1. Lay a ball down on the practice tee.

2. Stand behind it and sight a line from it to a distant target.

3. Place another ball on that line five or six feet in front of the original ball. Check from behind the original ball to make sure that the intermediate ball is on your target line.

4. Move into position alongside the original ball and set your club behind it, aimed carefully at the intermediate target. Do not look at your distant target as you aim the club.

5. Finally, look down your target line to see if your club appears to be aimed at your distant target.

If your clubface now appears to be aimed to the left of your distant target, you can assume that you tend to aim to the right of target on all of your shots, even putts. If it appears to be aimed to the right, you will know that you tend to aim to the left.

If you find that you have been misaiming badly, you should develop the habit of aiming at an intermediate target on all shots, both on the course and in practice. If you carefully spot-aim on each shot, you will begin to eliminate the swing compensations that you had been forced to make.

The rules do not allow you to drop another ball on your line during play, but you can select a blemish in the grass to use as your intermediate target.

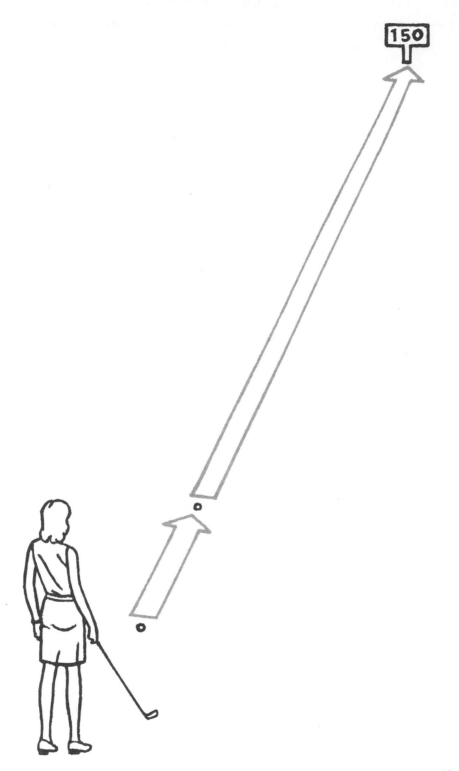

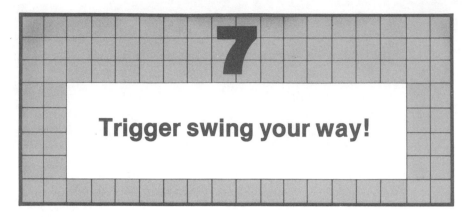

Trigger swing your way!

It is difficult to make a smooth and rhythmic golf swing from a rigid, static position. Good golfers develop some little preswing movement, some individual mannerism that helps break tension immediately before they begin the backswing.

The next time you watch golf on television try to detect what each player does just before his or her clubhead starts away from the ball.

It may be a slight inward kicking of the right knee—a move favored by Gary Player—or a tiny sliding of the hips to the left, or a cocking of the chin to the right, as in the case of Jack Nicklaus.

The specific type of move that you develop is immaterial, so long as you do something to trigger your swing.

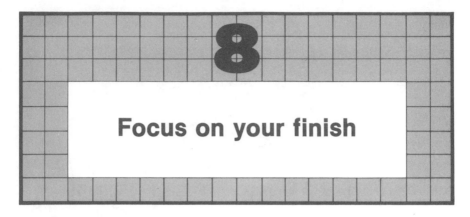

Focus on your finish

When you watch the tour professionals perform on television it becomes clear that golf is a game of finesse and self-control, rather than the unfortunate, earthshaking violence that all too many amateurs put into their swings.

Focus on how the pros appear at the finish of their swings on full shots. Usually they will be in excellent balance. They will seem to have complete control of their bodies.

This indicates they have swung the club at a pace they can control—that they have disciplined themselves to exert no more physical effort than they can transfer efficiently from club to ball.

You, too, can learn to swing within your personal limits of pace and effort, and thereby improve your shot-making. Start by studying how the pros look as they finish the swing. Then take a club out into the yard and make some full swings—no ball needed—from your normal address position.

Before each swing, imagine how you want to look and feel at the completion of the swing.

Once you can finish in balance every time, follow this same procedure when actually striking balls. Again, be sure to dwell on how you will finish each swing before you actually start to make it.

Swing into action A.S.A.P.

Start your swing A.S.A.P.—as soon as possible—after setting the clubhead behind the ball. Learn to pull the trigger before tension can set in and thwart your chances of making a full, rhythmic swing.

Set the clubhead behind the ball and then start counting to yourself. Settle into your address position and start your swing before you reach the count of five.

At first you may feel rushed, but soon you will train yourself to plan ahead and start your swing sooner, not only on practice shots but on the course as well.

10

Wind up slowly
to throw a strike

There is nothing to be gained, and much to be lost, by hurrying your backswing. Its purpose is simply to put yourself and your club into position to propel the ball forward. This does not require a great deal of effort or speed.

A rushed backswing causes you instinctively to grip the club too firmly. This tension quickly spreads up your arms and into your shoulders. It reduces the flexibility you need to turn fully and then swing the club through impact at your maximum speed. It also decreases your chance of applying the clubface squarely to the ball.

A good image to keep in mind is that of a baseball pitcher who slowly winds up and rears back to throw the ball forward at top speed. See that pitcher's windup in your mind's eye as you make your backswing. Soon you will begin to feel the pace of the backswing that you need for all your shots, from drives to putts.

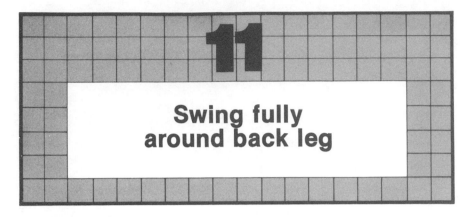

Swing fully around back leg

Do your shots with the longer clubs usually curve to the right? Do those that do not curve usually fly to the left of your target? Do you often find your weight is on your back foot at the end of your swing? Do you sometimes feel that you have lifted your upper body or looked up?

If this pattern sounds all too familiar, you should understand this:

While your weight *should* shift to the left foot during the downswing, it cannot if it has *remained* on that foot during the backswing.

Try swinging fully around your *right* leg during your backswing. Then give yourself time to shift your weight onto your left foot before you return the clubhead to the ball.

Do not be concerned if you feel that this makes you sway to the right during your backswing. Do not try to keep your head steady or down. Such efforts may, in fact, be the basic reason for your particular problems.

12

Use mirror to check backswing basics

Here's a way to be sure you are putting yourself and your club into positions that will let you apply force efficiently to the ball.

You will need a mirror in which you can see at least the upper part of your body when standing seven feet or farther away.

Take a club and set up to an imaginary ball, as if you were going to hit it *away* from the mirror. Stand far enough to make a backswing.

Grip the club and assume

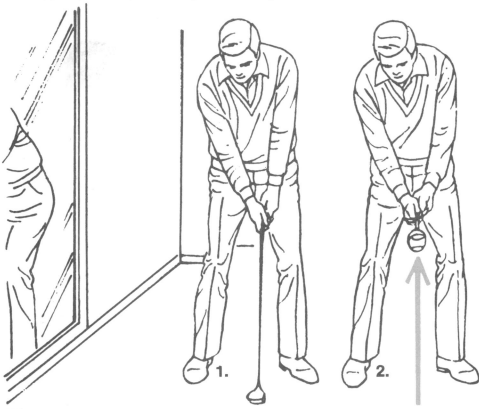

1.

2.

your address position (1). Then, *using only your hands and wrists,* raise the club *straight* up as far as you can (2). Do not lift your arms or straighten your legs or body. From this position, complete your backswing and hold position (3).

Check in the mirror to see if you and your club are in the positions listed below. Do so by merely turning your head toward the mirror. (Illustration 4 will help clarify the positions to be checked.)

1. Your left arm should be fairly straight—not rigid, but bent no more than a few degrees.

2. Your hands should ap-

pear in the mirror above your back shoulder.

3. The highest part of your hands should be higher than the top of your head.

4. Your clubshaft should be set much closer to horizontal than vertical.

5. Your clubshaft should extend more or less parallel to your target line.

Once you find the model position, swing to it repeatedly in front of the mirror. Each time sense how it feels to be in that position. Keep burning this sensation into your "muscle memory" until you can swing to it every time.

3.

4.

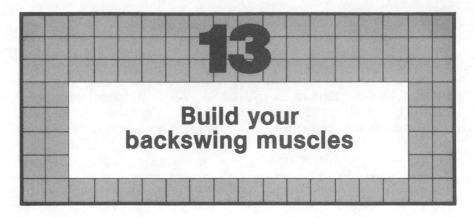

13

Build your backswing muscles

Much has been said about the importance of making a full backswing turn. Too little has been said about the muscular flexibility needed to make such a turn.

Here is a simple exercise to increase your flexibility.

Lie flat on the floor with your legs extended, your hands clasped under the back of your head and your elbows touching the floor.

Slowly move your right leg over your left as far as you can without your right elbow lifting from the floor. You will feel tension across your back and on the inner part of your right thigh.

Return your right leg to its original position and repeat the drill. You should find that this time you can move it even farther to the left without your right elbow leaving the floor.

Do this three or four times and then reverse the procedure, swinging your left leg over your right, making sure that your left elbow does not leave the floor.

Finally, swing the right leg over the left and then the left over the right in rapid succession several times, each time stretching as far as you can.

The drill will not take much more than a minute or two each day, but it will help make your hours on the golf course more productive.

14

Pause at top for better balance

Most golfers fly their shots farther and straighter when they give themselves an extra split second between backswing and downswing. They need this very slight pause to gather themselves together behind the ball, to regroup their muscles and stay in balance while changing directions.

You can make this pause a natural part of your swing by playing practice shots (1) with your feet together, or (2) on just one foot, right or left, or (3) with your left foot off the ground on your backswing.

As you apply any of these practice drills, try hitting the ball—but do not worry if you make a poor shot, or even miss the ball. The important thing is to sense the additional time that they force you to take between backswing and downswing.

1. 2. 3.

15

Snap your fingers to strengthen golf muscles

Most golfers could add distance and accuracy to their shots merely by doing one simple exercise each day. You can do it almost anywhere you have a little privacy.

This exercise increases the strength and elasticity of the muscles attached to the last three fingers of the left hand (right hand for left-handers). These muscles extend through the wrist and underside of the forearm. They are extremely important, both in controlling the moving club and in squaring its face to the intended line of play as it returns to the ball.

Simply extend the left arm and hand out to your side with the last three fingers together. Then snap those fingers inward quickly so they slap against the palm. Repeatedly open and close them as rapidly and forcefully as you can, for at least a minute or two.

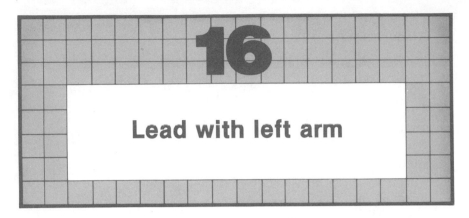

16

Lead with left arm

Golfers frequently play better after attending a professional tournament. Suddenly their swings feel more rhythmic and grooved. This is because we have the innate ability to mimic motion.

The next time you watch golf on television, focus your attention on each player's left arm as he or she swings. Observe the pace and rhythm of its movement. Absorb it. Feel the "beat" between backswing and forwardswing. Feel the left arm's forward swish, its gradual acceleration through the ball and beyond.

Your eventual success at golf will depend largely on your ability to swing your lead arm back and forward at a pace you can control and with a beat that never varies—from drives to approach shots to putts.

Trust your mind and body to translate the lead-arm motion you see on television into a pace and rhythm that works for you.

17

Steady head channels full swing's power

A steady head position is important for controlling the full, free swing. But the term "steady head" should not imply a rigid head. Your head may turn slightly in the direction your arms are swinging (see illustration). This turning of the head helps you swing freely.

What "steady head" does mean is that you should curtail excessive upward, downward or sideways shifting of the head as you swing, because shifting your head can throw your swing out of its proper path of movement, reducing your chances of making solid contact.

The perfectly steady head is an ideal that few golfers ever achieve, even top professionals. However, trying for a steady head leads to a *steadier* head.

18

Use your weight to help your swing

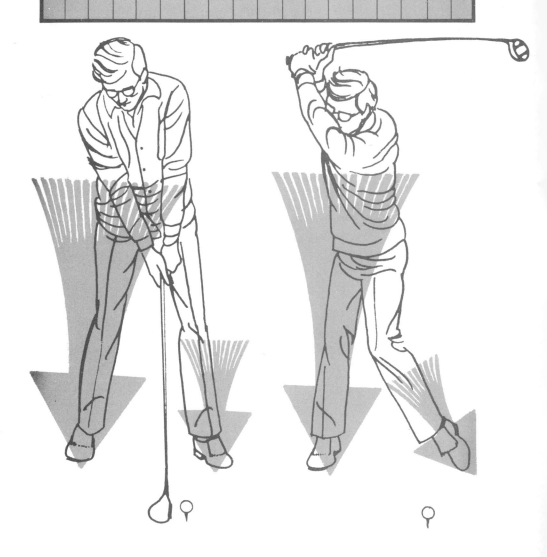

When making a full swing, good golfers finish with the weight largely on the left foot; poor players frequently fall back on the right foot (vice versa for left-handers).

To nip this problem from the start, set up for full shots with your weight primarily on your right foot. Keep it there during your backswing. Then simply move your knees to the left at the start of your downswing, and your weight will follow.

Starting with too much weight on the left foot, or shifting it there during the backswing, leads to a reverse weight shift to the right during the downswing. Mis-hit shots usually result.

II.
The Head
Game

Concentrate on one thing

Here is a quick and simple experiment that indicates how you should think when playing golf shots. All you need is a small table on which a few items are scattered.

Start by studying each item individually. Notice as many details about each as you can, but spend no more than three or four seconds on one item before shifting your vision to the next.

After you have studied all the items, immediately close your eyes and wait for an image to appear in the darkness. If one comes forth, retain it as long as you can.

Next, repeat the procedure, but this time focus only on one item. Do not look for details. Just stare at it as intensely as you can for at least 15 seconds. Now, close your eyes and wait for an image; hold it as long as you can.

Most who take this test not only see a much stronger image after intensely studying just one item; they also see the shape of other items as well, perhaps even the table itself.

It is much the same in golf. We make our best swings when our mind's eye has a clear idea of what we want to accomplish. Concentrating on a single thing before and during each swing—your target is an excellent choice—gives your mind a clear image. Thinking about too many things before and during the swing—"head down," "left arm straight," "avoid the trees on the left," etc.— merely creates a muddled image and a haphazard swing.

20

Learn to keep track of a target you cannot see

It is nighttime and you are standing at one edge of a large room next to a lighted lamp. The door leading from the room is at the other end. Various pieces of furniture sit between you and that door.

Your challenge is to switch off the lamp, darkening the room, and walk through the doorway at the other end without bumping into furniture or a wall along the way.

You focus on the doorway and the room's furniture. You decide on the path you will take. Your body senses how it will feel to walk that path.

Finally, you switch out the light and begin your walk. As you proceed, you continue to envision your goal. You imagine where the doorway is, both in terms of direction and distance from where you happen to be.

This cooperation of mind and body to reach a goal that you cannot see applies similarly in golf. As you swing the club, you cannot see your target, so before you swing you should focus on that target, checking both its direction and distance from your ball. As you swing you should retain that target image in your mind's eye, just as you would a doorway in a darkened room.

At first you may not succeed very often, just as you might bump into furniture, or at least walk hesitatingly, the first time you exit from a dark room.

But in time, after you have hit many golf shots, your sense of direction and distance will improve so that you can swing the club freely and stroke the ball correctly.

21

Play by feel

There is a sort of nirvana that a golfer occasionally achieves. The player knows beforehand, with absolute certainty, that he is going to make the exact shot that he wants to make. He actually senses how his upcoming swing will feel.

Expert players take this a step further. Rather than wait for this state of bliss to descend upon them, they actually create it through "playing by feel."

First they visualize the shot that they want to make. Then they summon forth the feeling of the swing they will need to produce that shot.

Finally, they merely duplicate that feeling as they swing.

Golfers who hope to eventually play by feel must develop a backlog of success patterns. To do this, make it a point to follow this two-step procedure whenever you play or practice:

1. Closely watch each good shot that you make. Watch how the ball flies, where it lands and what it does thereafter.

2. Reflect on how your swing felt. File that feeling away in your mind and body, just as you did the picture of the shot.

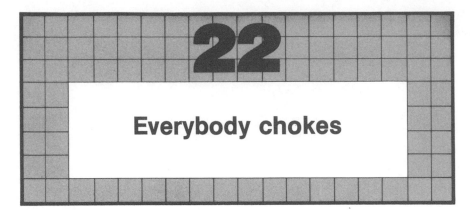

22

Everybody chokes

During your golfing career you will mis-hit many, many shots simply because your nerves were not up to the test.

This is nothing to be ashamed of, to worry about or to become discouraged over. Nervous tension has been the No. 1 foe of every great golfer who ever lived. They've all choked somewhere along the line. You will too.

There is no one big secret for controlling your nerves, but the more you put yourself into pressure situations, the better you'll become at handling them. So play with good golfers whenever possible and enter as many competitions as you can.

When you do feel the pressure mounting, merely hold the club lightly, focus full attention on where you want the shot to go and then simply give it your best possible swing.

Blame the game,
not yourself

One of the most consistent things about golf is its inconsistency. The sooner a golfer realizes this, the sooner he or she will begin to play better and enjoy the game more.

Understanding what makes playing more difficult than practicing should ease your frustration:

1. Playing is for keeps. Every shot counts. There are no second tries, a fact that inevitably increases tension and inhibits a free swing.

2. You cannot work into a groove on the course by swinging the same club shot after shot, as you can on the range.

3. On the course you may be hitting from sidehill lies.

4. On the course you are prey to such negative thoughts as hitting into trees, sand, water, etc., dubbing an easy shot, embarrassing yourself in front of others, making a high score.

Blaming oneself for bad shots merely creates unneeded tension that leads to more bad shots. Instead, blame them on the highly challenging nature of the game itself. Then meet that challenge by developing your skills through playing, practicing, taking lessons and studying successful golfers.

24

Minimize the consequences of bad shots by thinking ahead

Because golf is indeed a challenging game, to err is all too human, especially for the player who has not had time to develop his skills. However, by applying some simple, everyday logic to the game, even the beginner can greatly minimize the consequences of bad shots.

For instance, such logic should make it plain that:

- An imperfect drive does little harm so long as it finishes on the fairway instead of in deep rough, in sand or behind a tree.
- A poor shot to the green is less likely to create additional problems if the preceding shot has left your route to the flagstick free of such obstacles as trees, bunkers and water hazards.
- Except on short putts, any shot on the putting green can roll as much as two feet off line and not create a problem so long as it rolls the proper distance.

In short, focus your attention on driving into the fairway, positioning yourself for an open shot to the green and making your putts roll the right distance.

25

Set your personal "par"

Every golf hole has a designated "par," based primarily on length. Par is the number of strokes an expert should expect to take on the hole if he or she plays errorless golf, with no fluke shots, under normal weather conditions.

The men's and women's par figures are printed on the scorecard. Par for a hole includes two strokes for putts. Thus an expert playing well should expect to reach the green of a par-3 hole in one shot, a par 4 in two and a par 5 in three.

Golfers should set their own par standard. An adult male just starting the game might, for instance, try to average three shots per hole over the stated par. A woman or youngster might,

at first, attempt to average four over, or five over. As you improve you should lower your personal standard.

Setting your par in this fashion gives you something to shoot for, even when playing by yourself. It provides a measurement of your improvement. It also gives you incentive to keep plugging away, trying to maintain your average, by offsetting a high score on one hole with lower-than-average scores on succeeding holes.

Finally, playing against your own par will dramatically spotlight the importance of saving strokes, especially through improving your short-game skills on and around the greens.

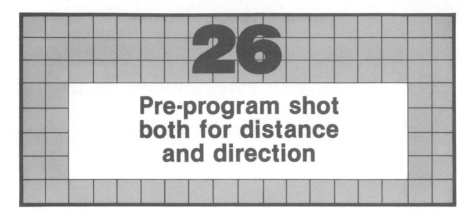

26

Pre-program shot both for distance and direction

Every golf shot presents you with two challenges. One is to make the ball go a certain direction. The other is to make it go a certain distance.

You'll have better results more often if you clear your mind by separating these two challenges as you prepare to make each shot.

First, stand behind the ball and select a target you feel sure you can reach. On putts and short approach shots it probably will be the flagstick or the hole itself. On longer shots to the green it may be a spot on the putting surface. On drives it will be a point in the fairway. Choose the club you feel will serve you best in strik-

ing the shot to that point.

Second, switch off "direction" for the moment and think only "distance." Make a rehearsal swing and try to program the amount of motion and force you will need to make the shot reach your target.

Third, switch on "direction" again. Set your clubhead behind the ball and aim it down your target line. Then set your feet and body parallel to that line.

When you are ready to make the shot, keep your direction beam on by checking your target again. Keep the target in your mind's eye and swing for distance by duplicating the feel of your rehearsal swing.

1. Think direction

2. Think distance

3. Think direction

4. Think distance

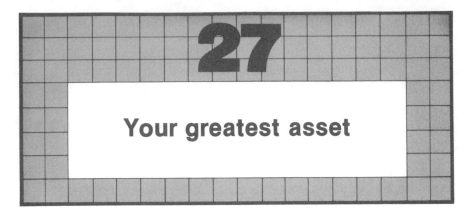

Your greatest asset

New golfers seldom use their greatest assets—their imaginations.

All great players have learned to visualize success. They see the shot they wish to play before they swing the club. In effect they "tell" their senses what they want to do. They rely on their sensory system to "tell" their muscles how to do it.

Gary Player once was observed on a practice green, putting over and over from only 18 inches. He was asked why he practiced so diligently on putts he obviously could sink without fail. "To make putts," he said, "you must learn to see the ball going into the hole beforehand. My subconscious is watching these putts go in."

Sam Snead frequently "plays golf" in his mind before he arrives at the course. He sees every drive fly long and straight. He sees every approach shot finish close to the hole.

"And," he adds, "in my imagination I never miss the putt."

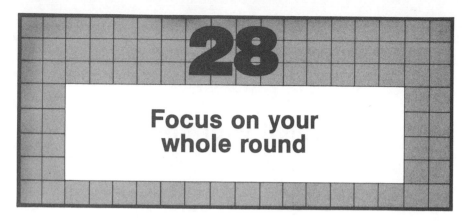

28

Focus on your whole round

Golfers take great pride in shooting a low score on one hole, as well they should.

Sooner or later, however, it is better to adjust your thinking toward shooting a good score for the full round, rather than a good score on each hole. This psychological step will help you avoid the emotional peaks and valleys that inevitably lead to trying too hard or giving up after a particularly bad hole, or letting down after a good one.

One way to focus on the whole round rather than its 18 parts is to first decide on a total score that is somewhat lower than you have ever shot before. Then try to complete as many holes as you can before reaching that total.

Each time you actually finish a full round in that number of strokes or fewer, readjust your 18-hole scoring goal to a lower number. Then, again try to play as far into the course as you can before taking that number of shots.

This same technique can be applied to nine-hole rounds if you do not normally play a full 18.

Watch your shots

There is much to be learned from every shot you make. The golfer who is aware of this and applies this awareness on every shot—in practice and on the course—builds a backlog of information that can make the difference between excellence and mediocrity in years to come.

Here are some of the things to be learned from watching your shots all the way to their finish:

- How high and far the ball flies when struck with different clubs.
- How the ball reacts when landing on different types of surfaces.
- How wind affects ball flight.
- How the lie of the ball in grass affects shots with different clubs.
- How any slope on which you are standing affects your shot.

- How your swing feels when you make a certain type of shot, good or bad.
- How your shots change with various alterations in your preswing and swing technique.

No one could consciously memorize all of these things. However, simply being aware of your golfing environment and watching your shots will cause subliminal learning. Your sensory system will backlog the information, storing it for the future when you will be asking yourself such questions as:

What club will I need to make the ball go over (or under) that limb? Can I reach the green with this club against this wind? How should my swing feel to make this shot curve around that tree? Which way will this shot curve from this slope?

III.
Focus
on Faults

Doing what comes unnaturally

In many ways golf is an unnatural game. The player whose shots skitter along the ground naturally tries to loft them higher by swinging upward to the ball. The player whose shots curve to the right of target naturally starts swinging more and more to the left. The player whose shots curve left swings more to the right.

In each case the seemingly natural remedy usually aggravates the problem.

The drawings below show

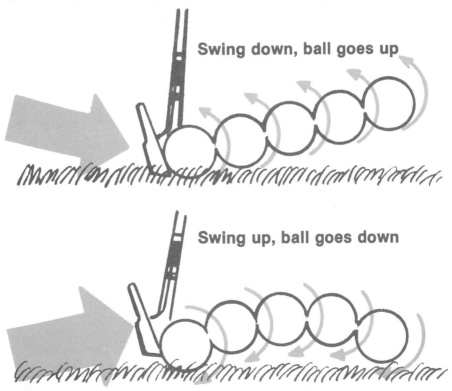

Swing down, ball goes up

Swing up, ball goes down

how clubhead path affects ball spin. By understanding these principles you will be able to apply proper, though perhaps unnatural, corrections.

Top left: A slightly *descending* blow puts backspin on the ball on iron shots so that they will *ascend* and remain airborne a normal duration. (A level, sweeping blow creates sufficient backspin on wood shots.)

Bottom left: Swinging upward to hit shots *higher* reduces backspin —or applies topspin—so that they fly *lower.*

Top right: Swinging to the left to avoid slicing to the right usually adds clockwise spin to the ball. It curves even farther to the right.

Bottom right: Swinging to the right to avoid hooking to the left usually adds counterclockwise spin. The ball hooks even more drastically to the left.

The best way to hit your shots straight and high and far is with the clubhead moving toward your target at impact, descending slightly on iron shots and sweeping level on wood shots.

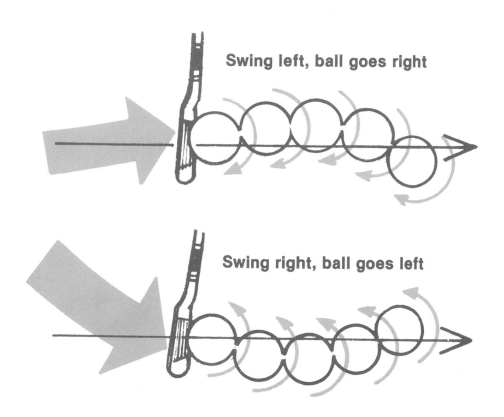

Swing left, ball goes right

Swing right, ball goes left

31

Brush imaginary spot with club

A major challenge for most golfers is getting the ball up in the air well enough on full shots. The clubhead often contacts the top of the ball and sends it dribbling along the ground, usually off to the left.

Concentrate on swinging the club freely through the ball with your arms, allowing your wrists to uncock as a result. It may help you contact the bottom of the ball if you will focus on a spot some two inches behind the ball, rather than on the ball itself. Try to brush the grass at that spot as you swing the club freely down and forward with your arms.

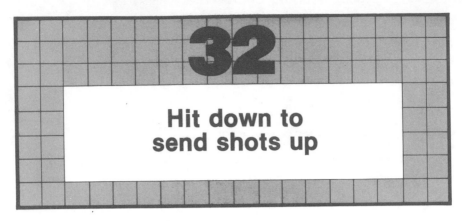

Hit down to send shots up

Golfers should understand that their clubs have been especially designed to make the ball fly into the air. The upward facing of the club-head—its "loft"—accomplishes this aim.

Those golfers who don't appreciate this fact invariably try to hit or scoop the ball upward with their swings. Their efforts usually cause the clubhead to be moving upward when it reaches the ball. Its sharp leading edge knifes into the back side of the ball and sends it scooting along the ground (top drawing)—and often the ball's cover is cut.

This exasperating and expensive result becomes even more likely when the ball rests low in the grass or on bare ground. Then the temptation to scoop it upward is even greater, and the low-lying ball is even more susceptible to being "skulled" by an upward-moving club-head.

The remedy is to use your clubs as the manufacturer intended and strike the ball with a slightly downward-moving clubhead (except when it sets up on a wooden tee). Then the clubface can contact the underside of the ball (second drawing) and the built-in loft can send it upward.

As a general rule, the lower your ball rests in the grass, the steeper your angle of approach must be to assure solid contact.

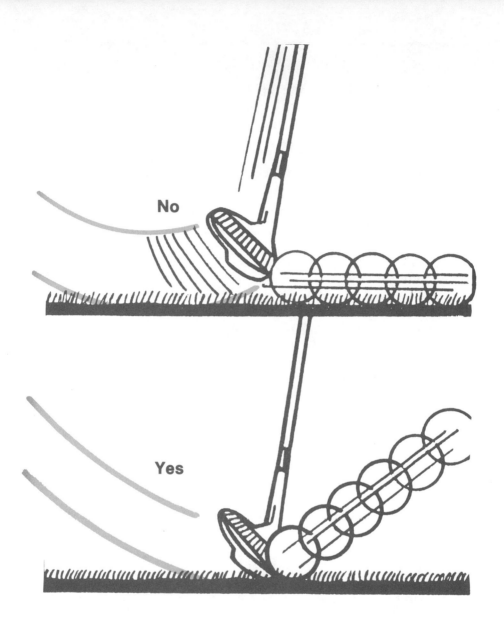

No

Yes

Lofted club straightens tee shots

If your long shots usually slice from left to right, you should take steps to correct the problem's basic cause as soon as possible. Until you can master the correction, however, you can minimize the slice by driving with a No. 3 or No. 4 wood rather than the No. 1 wood.

Since the higher-numbered woods are more lofted, they tend to make initial contact lower on the back side of the ball (see illustration). The lower contact creates more backspin, which offsets at least some of the slice-producing sidespin. Shots will curve to a lesser degree.

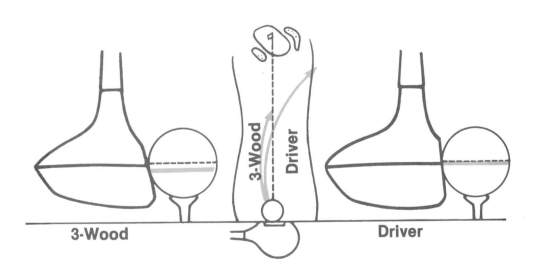

3-Wood   3-Wood   Driver   Driver

34

How to slow down your swing

Virtually all golfers have the unfortunate tendency to swing too fast at times. Even the touring pros fall victim occasionally.

The poor shot that usually results from quick swinging is bad enough, and the problem becomes even more insidious if the golfer fails to realize that he swung too fast. He may blame the bad shot on some other cause and self-prescribe the wrong "cure." In trying to consciously alter his technique on the next shot, the player often will create additional tension that makes him swing still faster.

To determine whether it was swinging too fast that caused you to mis-hit a shot, merely reflect on how your swing felt. Specifically, try to recall having made a backswing. If you can't remember any backswing sensations, you probably swung too fast.

In that case, take two or three practice swings before you play your next full shot. On each, swing your arms back and forward as fully and as freely as you can but slowly enough to retain your balance. Sense how your arms feel as they swing. Try to recreate that same feeling as you play the actual shot.

Relax right arm to reduce slicing

If your shots often slice from left to right or pull to the left of your target, the reason may be too much tension in your right hand and arm.

As you address the ball, your right arm should feel soft and ready to fold during your backswing. Hold the club lightly in your right hand and a bit firmer in the last three fingers of your left. Try to maintain that same grip pressure throughout your entire swing.

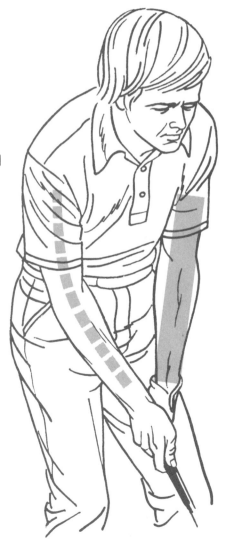

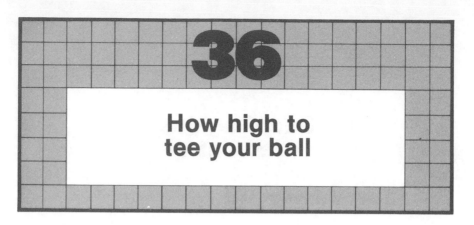

36

How high to tee your ball

If you are not sure how high to set the ball on tee shots with wood clubs, a good norm is to make sure that the equator of the ball is even with the top of the clubface when the club is resting on the ground behind it.

If you have found that on many of your tee shots the club chops down under the ball and pops it ineffectively upward, avoid the temptation to tee the ball lower than normal to avoid undercutting it. Teeing it low will merely increase your tendency to chop downward.

Instead, tee it higher than normal—at least during practice sessions. Then your subconscious reaction will be correct—you will automatically begin to sweep the ball away with the clubhead moving level or slightly upward at impact.

If you have found that your tee shots often fly very low from right to left—or you may find it difficult to get the ball airborne with your 1-wood—resist the temptation to tee the ball higher than normal. This would merely strengthen your tendency to swing on a relatively flat plane.

Instead, practice hitting shots with your 3-wood or 4-wood from a tee set lower than normal. This will force you to begin swinging on a more upright plane to make solid contact.

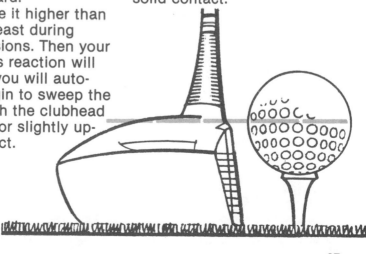

Guard against overcontrol

Most golfers do not swing the club as freely as they should. Instead they over-control it with their hands. Either they hold it too tightly from the start or they grab it at some point in the swing.

The result of this overcontrol is tension, a tightening of muscles that inhibits clubhead speed and square contact.

The tendency to overcontrol the club usually starts early in one's golfing career.

After mis-hit or whiffed shots, it is natural to hold the club tighter in an effort to guide it back to the ball.

You will develop your potential to contact the ball solidly with maximum clubhead speed only if you swing your arms freely with a light grip pressure that remains more or less constant throughout your stroke. Try to get the feeling you're swinging a feather.

A one-hand drill
for slicers

If your golf shots slice off to the right, you are probably overcontrolling the club with your hands.

Work with a drill that star teaching professional Bob Toski often uses with his pupils. Practice hitting short shots—no more than 20 paces—with only your right hand on the club, and with the ball teed.

Do this until you consistently can strike the ball solidly and it feels light com-ing off the clubface. You will find this all but impossible to do with a tight grip.

Thereafter, play these short shots with both hands on the club, maintaining the same, constant light grip pressure.

Do not hit longer shots until you can make solid contact consistently with both hands on the club at this distance. Return to the right-hand-only drill if your slicing tendency recurs.

39

Swing from inside to tame slice

In golf it is human nature to swing the club in a way that we sense will offset our past shotmaking errors. This natural tendency can become extremely detrimental for those golfers who happen to slice their shots to the right (first drawing).

When their shots continually finish to the right, these players unconsciously begin swinging more and more to the left (second drawing).

Swinging to the left tends to increase the amount of left-to-right sidespin applied to the ball (third drawing).

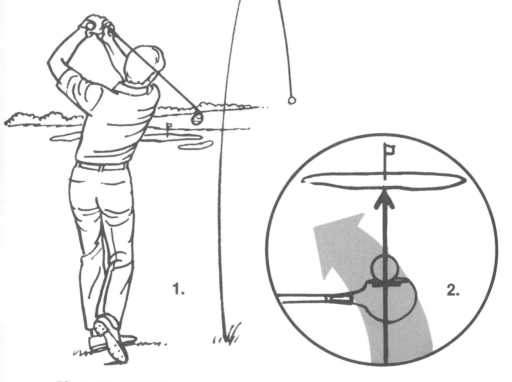

1.

2.

This increases the curve of the shot and decreases its length.

Moreover, swinging to the left steepens the downward path of the clubhead (fourth drawing) and further reduces the ball's forward progress.

All of these initial reactions to slicing become more pronounced with time. Soon the player has developed an inefficient swing pattern that may last for life.

To overcome this slice-inducing pattern, concentrate on swinging the club from *inside* the target line *straight down the path* toward the target. At the same time, your forearms should rotate counter-clock-wise on the forward swing and the hands should be allowed to release or uncock through the impact area. This squares up the club-face, actually causing the toe of the club to be passing the heel as you make contact. Then your shots will fly straight or even curve from right to left.

Often a slight grip change—turning your hands farther to the right on the club at address—will help produce this right-to-left pattern, as long as your swing path is going straight down the line. Holding the club lightly in your right hand throughout the swing will help accomplish the release you need.

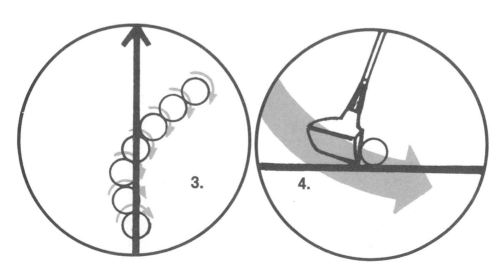

3.   4.

40

Help for the minority that hooks

While many right-handed golfers slice their long shots from left to right, some players have the opposite problem. Their shots, especially with the woods and longer iron clubs, curve to the left on a relatively low trajectory.

This happens because the club meets the ball while facing to the left of the path on which it is moving (first drawing). It has "closed" to the left too soon. This closing not only hooks the ball off-line, but also reduces the loft on the clubface. Hitting shots high enough into the air with a driver becomes all but impossible.

Usually this premature closing of the clubface results from a faulty grip. The golfer grips the club with his hands turned too far to his right. Turning them more to the left—more counterclockwise—will often solve the problem (second drawing).

If this grip alteration causes your long shots to start curving to the right, merely modify the degree of change.

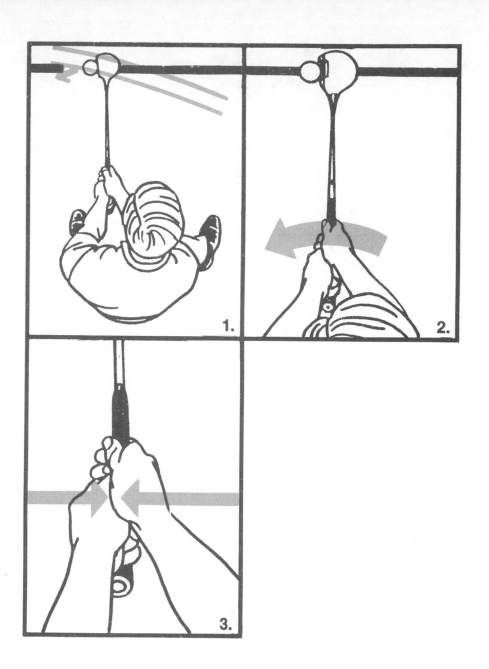

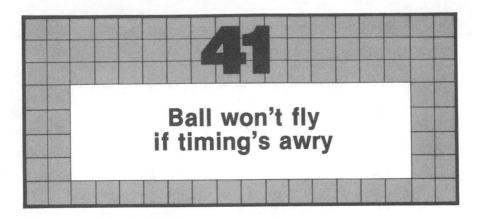

Ball won't fly
if timing's awry

Many golfers have the problem of hitting shots that barely get off the ground. Sometimes the club catches the ground behind the ball. More often it contacts only the top of the ball.

Hitting behind the ball usually means that your arms and hands are swinging the club down to it too soon. Give your arms a bit more backswing so that your left leg and hip have ample time to shift direction and clear to the left on the downswing.

Conversely, topping the ball usually means that your arms are not swinging downward soon enough. In this case you should focus on swinging the club freely through the bottom of the ball with your arms.

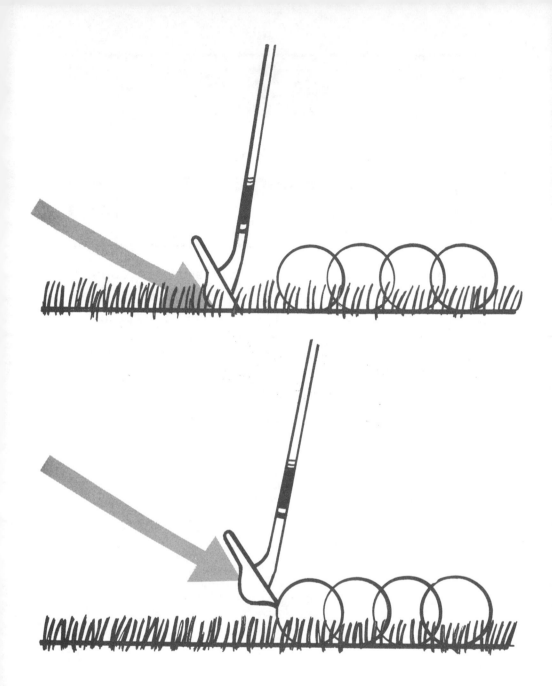

Keep your shoulders from ruining shots

In an effort to make the ball go farther, many golfers unconsciously become too aggressive with their shoulders. They actually lose distance because excessive shoulder action reduces clubhead speed at impact and causes glancing blows.

A simple way to learn if your shoulders are too active is to hit some practice shots with your feet together, actually touching each other. Try it with a 5-iron or a 6-iron and with the ball teed. Stick with this drill even if you mis-hit your first several shots.

If you make better contact than when your feet were apart, you will know that your shoulders tend to dominate your swing.

In that case, continue hitting shots with the ultra-narrow stance and try to sense how freely your arms are swinging. Also, identify the rhythm and pace at which they are moving. Then gradually widen your stance, but continue to swing your arms just as you did with your feet together.

Return to this drill whenever you start mis-hitting shots.

Free swinging comes first

The golfer who is seriously trying to develop a good game often becomes overly concerned about the mechanical specifics of the backswing. He may try to swing the club a certain length, or he may try to turn his left shoulder a certain way, or keep his left arm straight, or set his wrists in a certain way.

Usually these efforts reduce freedom of motion and take the player's mind away from his goal, which is simply to drive the ball toward a given target.

Here's a good drill for recapturing the free leg and body motion proper to an effective and power-producing swing.

First, without a club in your hands, assume your normal stance. Be sure you bend from the hips with your legs slightly flexed, but this time merely let your arms dangle (1).

Now swing your arms freely back and forward. As you swing your arms back, let your forward knee follow them—let it turn and slide toward your back leg (2). As you swing your arms forward, let your knees turn and slide toward your target (3). Continue swinging your arms and knees back and forth until you can feel them working together, without a club or ball. You should feel almost all of your weight on your rear foot at the top of your backswing, then on your forward foot during your forwardswing.

By now you should be finishing your forward swing with your body facing toward your target. Your rear knee should be pointing at the target, with your rear foot up on its toe (3).

If you are not finishing in this position, accentuate your weight shift onto your forward foot during your forward swing. Be aggressive. Swish your arms and legs forward.

Lengthier clubs take longer

Golfers frequently find that their drives do not go too much farther than, say, their 4-iron shots. Many players also slice their long shots to the right.

Both problems can result from swinging the longer-shafted clubs too fast. We sense that we must swing them faster to get the distance we know they are supposed to create.

You should understand that more time is needed to swing a longer-shafted club correctly. The clubhead of a driver, for instance, travels roughly five feet—or 30 percent—farther during the backswing and downswing than the clubhead of an 8-iron.

Allow yourself this extra time. You automatically will create more clubhead speed where it really matters—at impact. You also will give the clubface the time it needs to square itself to your target line at impact.

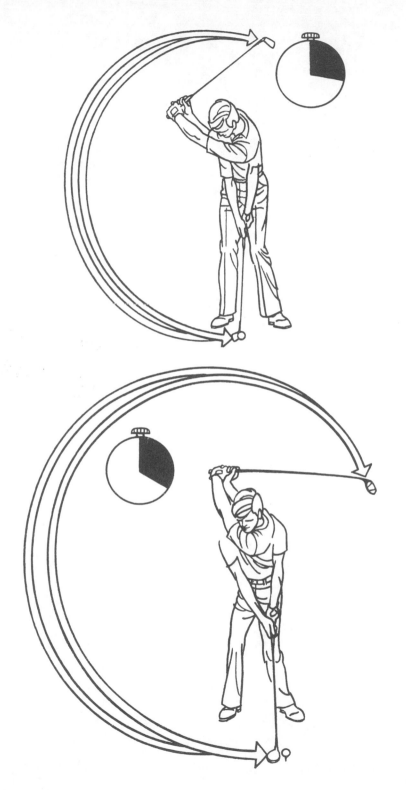

IV.
On-Course
Tactics

Plan your "trip"

Some golf holes are wide open and straightaway. Playing one of these is much like driving on a turnpike; you merely play down the open lane.

Most holes, however, include trouble areas to be avoided. Playing these holes is like trying to get to a small town by way of country roads. You should map out your "trip" before you start. Decide on a route that will take you to a point from where you can safely reach the next junction, eventually arriving at your final destination—the green.

If you run into a roadblock along the way, you will have to modify your travel plans. You will need to look for a detour that is sure to bring you back to civilization.

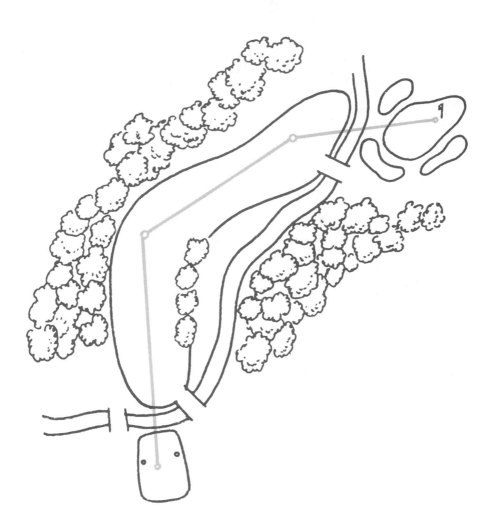

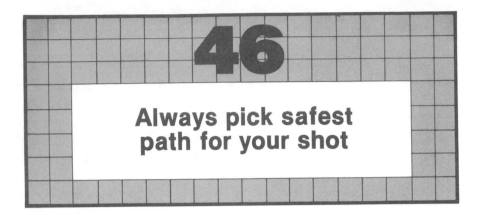

46

Always pick safest path for your shot

Until you become a highly proficient shotmaker, you can dramatically improve your scores by following one clear-cut guideline.

When you find your ball in a troublesome spot, such as in deep grass or behind trees or bushes, merely play a safety shot back into the fairway.

Choose a safe route and shoot to a spot along it that leaves you clear sailing for your next shot.

This ploy may cost you yardage for the moment, but over the course of a round it will save you strokes that you would waste trying to produce shots beyond your current level of skill.

47

Straight drives, even if short, get you there faster

Some golfers thrive on driving the ball past everyone else's tee shot. The rest wish they had that ability.

Without demeaning the obvious advantage of long driving, there is still much to be said for consistently driving a shorter distance in the right direction.

The goal on most drives is not to make the ball finish a great distance from the tee. Rather, it is to make the ball finish a *shorter* distance from the green.

The accompanying illustration is a good one to keep in mind. It shows that a ball driven 200 yards down the middle may finish closer to the target than a 220-yard drive that strays off line.

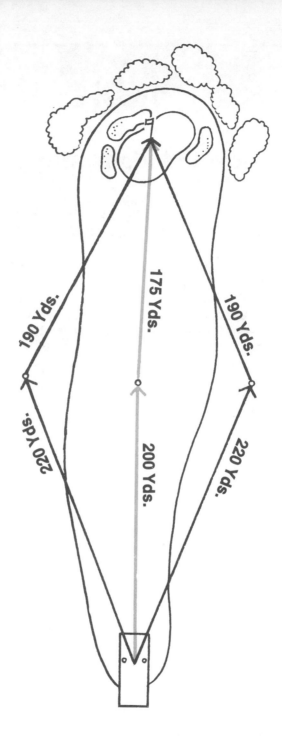

175 Yds.

190 Yds.

190 Yds.

200 Yds.

220 Yds.

220 Yds.

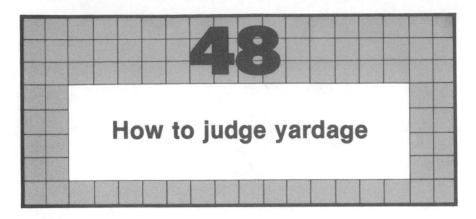

How to judge yardage

At a recent Golf Digest Instruction School, 10 pupils were taken to the tee of a par-3 hole. A yardage sign next to the tee indicated 124 yards from that spot to the center of the green, where the flagstick had been placed.

However, the tee markers were set back exactly 22 yards from the yardage sign, or 146 yards from the flagstick. Each student was

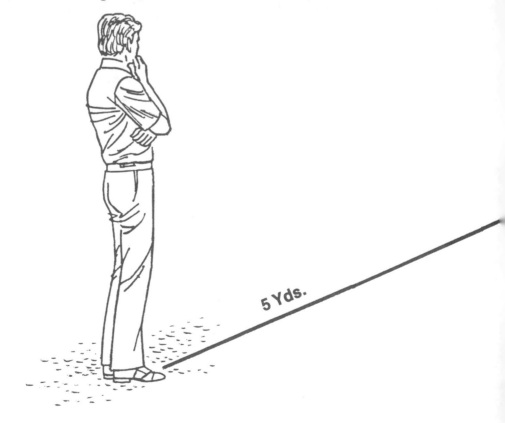

5 Yds.

asked to estimate how far the tee markers were behind the sign. The answers ranged from 15 to 33 yards.

In effect, if each student were to hit a shot the exact distance that he thought the hole measured, some would have wound up as much as seven yards short of the cup or 11 yards beyond.

All agreed that they would prefer not to leave themselves with putts of up to 33 feet after making a perfect shot.

Here's an easy way to learn to judge how far your ball sits from a yardage sign on the tee or from a 150-yard marker along a fairway. Take a handful of balls and start pacing outward from a tree, perhaps one in your yard. Drop a ball after every five steps you take. Then look back from each ball and "memorize" how far away the tree should look when it is, in fact, five yards, 10, 15, 20, etc., from your ball.

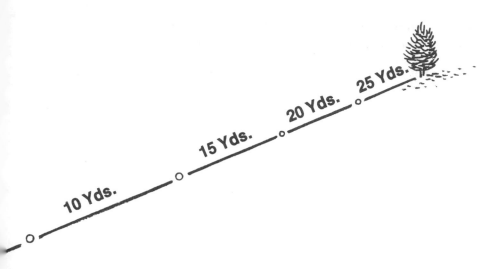

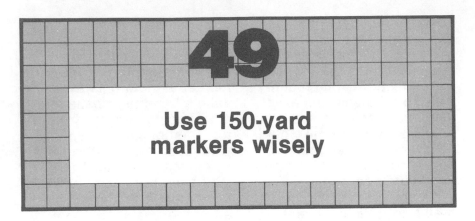

Use 150-yard markers wisely

Most golf courses include some sort of 150-yard indicator on longer holes—usually a bush or small tree alongside the fairway—to guide the player in selecting a club for his approach shot.

But many golfers misuse the indicators and mislead themselves.

Some fail to realize that the remaining 150 yards is measured from the *center* of the fairway opposite the indicator to the *center* of the green (line AB in drawing). They fail to add or subtract the yards that the flagstick is positioned from the center of the green (lines BD and BC respectively). And they fail to add yards when their ball rests far to the side of the fairway (line BE).

Also, many players misjudge the distance between the ball's actual position and the 150-yard point in the fairway (lines AF and AG). Individuals within a given foursome may judge these distances—shown here at 25 yards—to be anywhere from 15 to 35 yards.

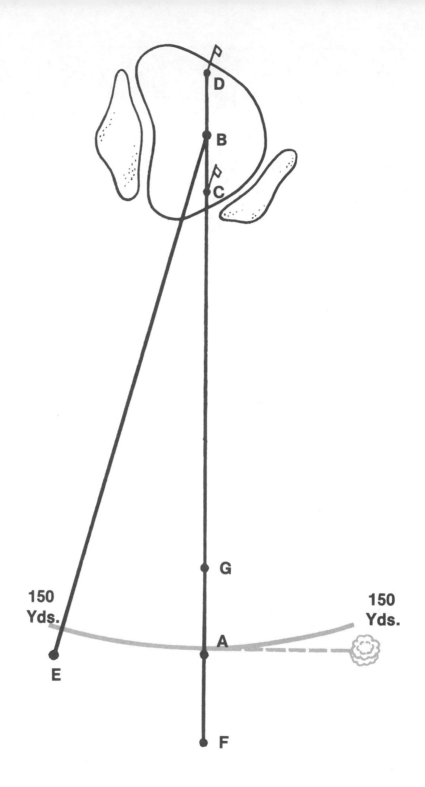

50

Approach with club that suits height of green

On many golf holes you will find that the green sits on ground that is higher or lower than the level from where you must play your approach shot.

The drawing shows how the height of a green affects the distance your approach shot flies before it lands.

When the green sits on higher ground, its surface interrupts the forward flight of the ball before it can travel a normal distance. When the green is on a lower level, the shot carries beyond its normal length before touching down.

Thus the height of the green becomes a factor to consider when deciding which club to use. If you have a shot of normal 6-iron length, you probably will need a 5-iron to reach a green that is above your level, or a 7-iron when it is below your level.

Here's a good way to remember this relationship: "Higher greens, lower-numbered clubs; lower greens, higher-numbered clubs."

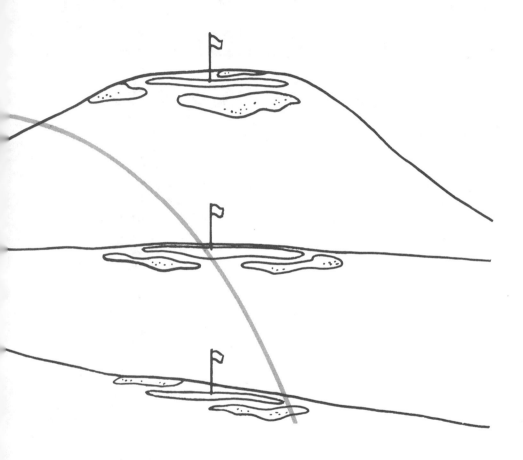

51

Club yourself realistically

Success at golf depends largely on being realistic with yourself.

After your next round, reflect back on where your full-swing shots to the greens actually finished. Count how many went too far. Count how many finished short. If you find that most came up short, ask yourself these two questions:

"Am I making these shots with clubs that I think will take my ball to the hole if I make a perfect shot?"

"How many times do I make a perfect shot?"

If your answers indicate that perhaps your expectations are exceeding your ability, try a different tack the next time you play.

Instead of choosing the club that would take your ball to the hole with a perfect shot, select the club that would take it to the back of the green but not over it.

If you are typical of the vast majority of golfers, you will find more of your shots finishing closer to the hole.

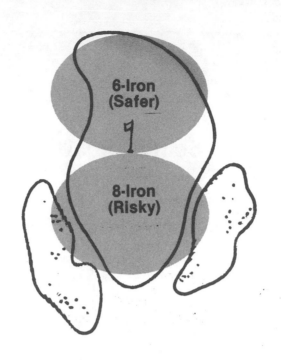

6-Iron
(Safer)

8-Iron
(Risky)

52

Scout ahead

Your ball rests near a green that is higher than your head. Thus from alongside the ball you cannot see what lies between the top of the slope and the flagstick.

This is a common situation, and one that often appears to be more difficult than it really is. From the ball it may seem that the area between the slope and the hole is so small that a shot landing there would run far past the cup. You may be misled into playing a risky shot to land on the slope or just barely beyond.

In this situation, so long as you do not delay play, you should scout ahead to determine just how much ground actually exists between the slope and your target. Usually there will be more than you had thought. You may be able to plan a safer shot— one that will readily clear the slope yet still stop near the hole.

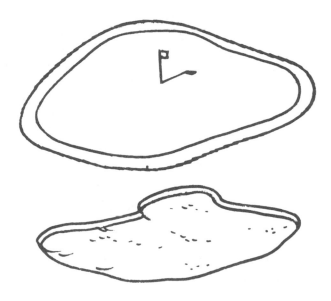

Check out yardage estimates

Many golf holes are deceiving. They appear to be longer or shorter than they really are. Frequently, for instance, an indiscernible dip in the fairway will make the flagstick seem closer than it really is.

One way to avoid being deceived is to follow the approach shot of a fellow player. Watch the ball in flight, determining in your own mind where you think it will land.

If it lands near that spot, you will know that your eyes are giving you the correct message on that particular hole. On your upcoming approach shot you can choose the club your eyes tell you to use.

If, however, your fellow player's shot lands well short of where you had thought it would, you will know that the hole is playing longer than it appears. Choose more club than you think you need, say a 5-iron instead of a 6.

On the other hand, if the ball you are watching lands well beyond the spot you had anticipated, you will know that the hole is playing shorter than it looks. Choose less club than you might have thought necessary.

V.
Chipping and Pitching

54

Play all short shots with mini-swing

Whenever your ball finishes on or near the green, your next shot almost always calls for a swing that is less than full—a mini-swing. Mini-swing shots are important in making a good score. A good player will make a mini-swing on more than half of his total shots.

There are three basic categories of mini-swing shots. Here's what they are and when to use them:

1. Pitch shots are played to the green. The ball flies relatively high, lands on the putting surface and settles quickly to a halt.

2. Chip shots also are played to the green, but usually with a less-lofted club. The ball flies low, lands just a few feet onto the putting surface and then bounces and rolls to the hole.

3. Putts are usually played on the green. They roll across the putting surface, hopefully into the hole.

To make solid contact more frequently it is best to putt when conditions permit, and better to chip than to pitch if the situation allows.

In general, putt the ball when it is on the green or just a few feet off the edge, providing it isn't nestled down, and the intervening grass is short and smooth.

Chip the ball when you have enough putting surface between you and the hole.

Pitch the ball and land it near the hole when there is too little putting surface to make a chip shot stop in time.

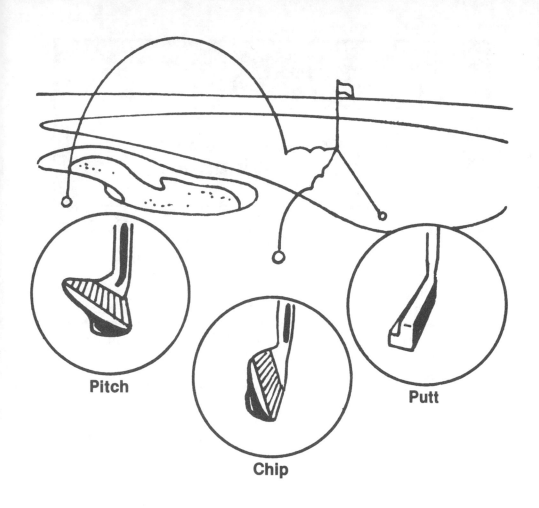

Pitch

Chip

Putt

Short shots require more imagination

The term "short game" refers to putts on the green and to shots played from nearby with a less-than-full swing.

Those who excel at golf realize the tremendous impact these shots have on their overall scores, and devote a large portion of their practice time to them. You should, too.

Resist the tendency of so many players to start preparing for another shot before the previous one has stopped rolling.

The short game is a game of imagination. Your long-term success on these shots will depend largely on how well you can anticipate beforehand just how far a given shot will fly, bounce and roll with a given amount of swing motion with a given club. Only by watching your shots to their finish can you build this vital backlog of knowledge.

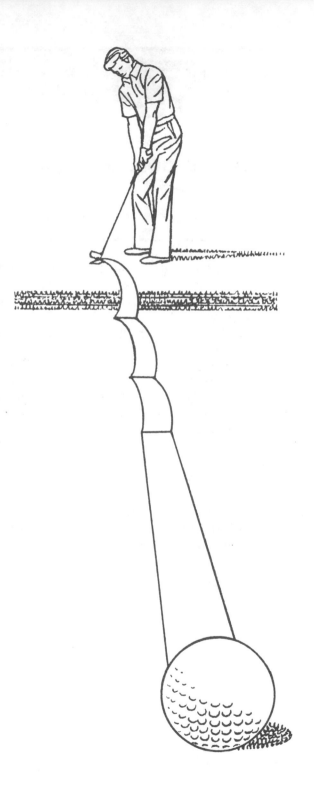

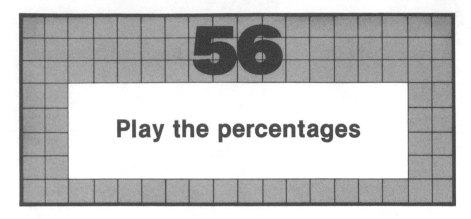

Play the percentages

Golfers who are confused about which clubs to use on short shots from just off the green can learn a great deal by watching the pros play these strokes.

You will note that whenever possible they try to land the ball on the smooth putting surface. Also, when possible they will play a low, running shot rather than a high, soft floater that carries farther but settles to a halt sooner.

They know that the low shot with a less-lofted club is easier than the high shot with a more-lofted iron.

As the player prepares to make one of these short shots, you should guess where he will try to land the ball and on what trajectory he'll make it fly.

If you guess wrong, try to figure out why he played a different shot. Perhaps he lacked sufficient space on the green to play a running shot, or he preferred to pitch the ball onto a more level landing area.

With practice you will learn what type of short shot to play in various situations and what club to choose.

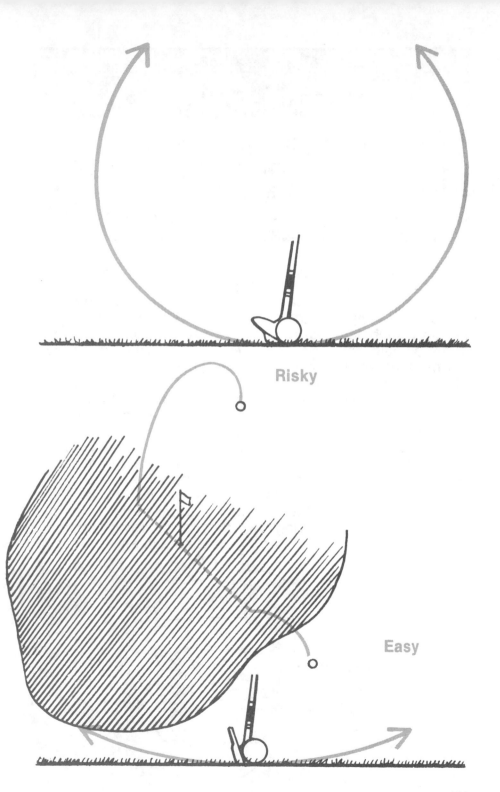

Risky

Easy

57

For higher pitch shots, hit "through the handle"

A pitch shot to the green is made with a highly lofted club such as a 9-iron or a wedge. It is supposed to fly relatively high, land softly and stop quickly.

Unfortunately, many golfers get just the opposite result. Despite the loft of the club, their shots fly too low and run too far.

The problem occurs if the clubhead reaches the bottom of its swing arc well behind the ball. By the time it finally reaches the ball, the club has already started moving upward. It makes contact too high on the ball.

If you have this problem, try the following:

Set your golf bag on the ground with its handle up, a few yards in front of where you will be hitting your practice shots (see illustration).

With your 9-iron or wedge, play the ball a bit farther back in your stance. Swing through the ball in a way that you think will make it go low and through the handle of the bag. After a few attempts to make the ball fly low, you will begin to feel the type of descending stroke needed to actually make it fly high.

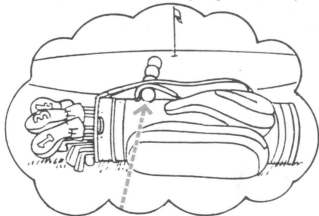

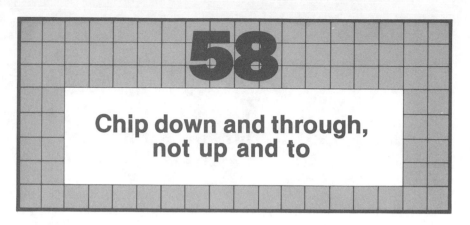

58

Chip down and through, not up and to

On those little chip shots from just off the green, most golfers try to guide the clubhead carefully up to the ball, hoping to loft it gently onto the putting surface.

In contrast, experts play chip shots with the clubhead accelerating slightly downward through the ball.

They trust the loft on the club to fly the ball up and forward with the downward-moving stroke.

To build trust in the technique as you practice, position a second ball about 10 inches behind the one you intend to contact. With your weight primarily on your forward foot, accelerate your arms downward and forward so that your clubhead passes over the trailing ball and down and through the one you are hitting.

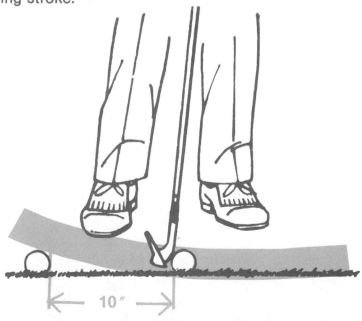

10"

59

Limit your arsenal

It is not coincidental that many of golf's finest players began the game with only a few clubs, some with only one or two. With such limited arsenals they were forced to develop a high degree of versatility that later gave them a vast repertoire of shots.

You can learn from their example. Scatter your golf balls at random distances around a practice green or a backyard target. From wherever these balls happen to settle, play them to your target with a single club, say an 8-iron, 9-iron or pitching wedge. Try to make some of your shots fly no higher than your knees or hips. Try to make some fly higher than your chest or head. But try to make them all finish at or near your target.

Almost immediately you will begin to discover what types of shots are easy, difficult or impossible from different distances and types of lies. You will begin to develop a sense of feel for distance. You will begin to visualize your intended shot before you play it, and develop the skill to play the shot you have visualized.

60

Chip like you putt

Apart from choosing a different club, you need to make
only two departures from
your basic putting technique

when playing chip shots:
1. You need not crouch
quite so much or position
your eyes directly over the

1.

2.

flight path. Do, however, crouch and grip down on the club more than you would for a full shot (1). This will give you better control of the clubhead.

2. Set most of your weight on your forward foot at address and keep it there as you swing your arms back and forth. Try to make the same arm stroke as in putting (2).

On chip shots land the ball just far enough on the green to assure that it won't catch in the longer grass. The goal is minimum carry through the air and maximum roll on the green. The iron club you select for the shot is the one that will best satisfy this goal and keep the ball from rolling far past the hole (3).

A few minutes in the backyard each day chipping balls into a container—a wastebasket or a cardboard box—with different clubs from different distances will improve your skill at making chip shots land at a certain spot and run to the hole.

3.

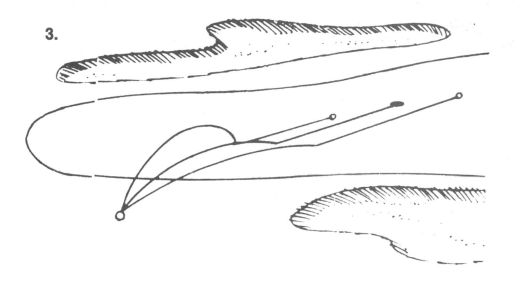

Keep wrist firm through impact

Many golfers waste strokes on short shots from around the green. More often than not, the ball never gets off the ground or darts over the green on an extremely low trajectory.

If you have this problem, check your left wrist and your clubhead at the finish of the stroke. If you find that the back of the wrist has cupped inward and the club-head has finished well above waist high (top illustration), you will know that your right hand is the culprit. It flipped the club upward into the ball, making the contact occur too high on its back side.

The correction is simply to subordinate the right hand's influence and allow a *downward* approach of the clubhead. Merely focus on finishing the stroke with your clubhead low to the ground and with your left wrist still uncupped (bottom illustration).

Practice without a ball until you can duplicate this finish position. This will train your left hand to control the club as your left arm leads and paces your forward stroke. You will be surprised how much crisper your shots will be when struck with a downward-moving clubhead.

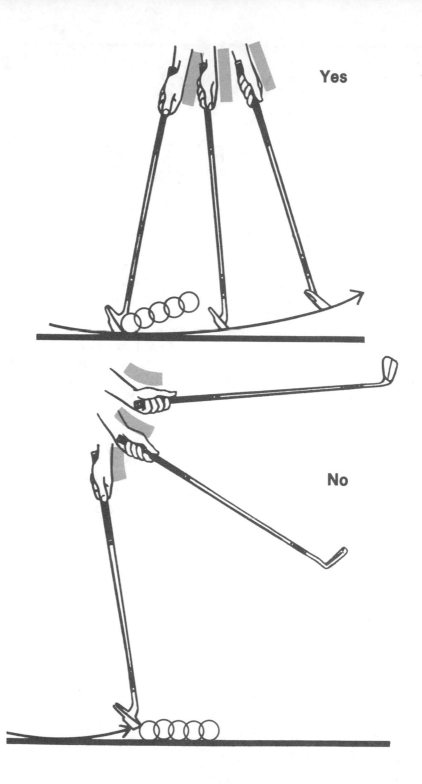

Yes

No

62

Make pitch shot with accelerating club

For the pitch shot, the only major departures in technique are in where you grip the club, set your feet and distribute your weight at address (1).

Since you are making a mini-swing, you can set your feet closer together than on a full swing with the same club, yet maintain your balance as you swing. By setting your forward foot a bit farther from your target line than your rear foot, you'll have more room to swing your arms freely forward. Take care in opening your stance to keep your shoulders parallel to your target line.

Avoid the natural tendency to slow down your forward swing just because you happen to be making a short shot. You will tend to decelerate your forward swing if your backswing is too long. The mini-swing is shorter going back, yet still rhythmic, with a distinct "one-and-two" beat (2).

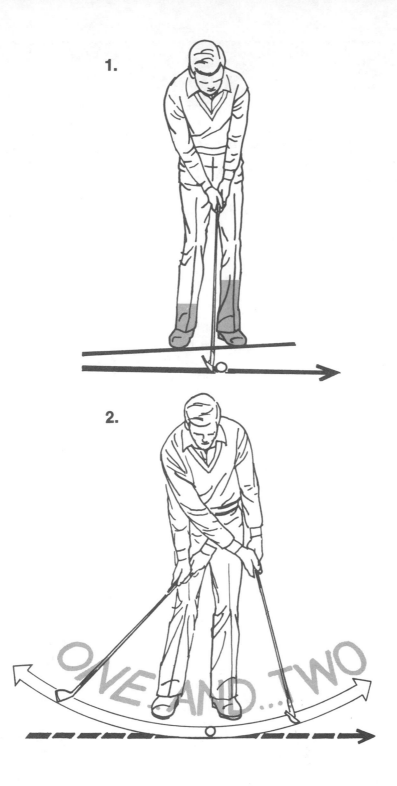

1.

2.

ONE AND...TWO

Try the penny-pinching pitch

If your short pitch shots with wedges and 9-irons fly lower than you'd like, or if some fly low and others high, try this practice trick.

Bring a few pennies with you to the practice tee and before you hit each shot place a coin two or three inches in front of the ball. Address the ball and swing as you normally would, but try to catch the penny with your clubhead after hitting the ball.

To contact the coin, you will be forced to "pinch" the ball with the clubhead while it is still moving downward, prior to reaching the bottom of its arc. This slightly descending blow is what you need on these shots, both for consistently crisp contact and for applying the backspin that helps make the ball fly higher.

64

Choke down for more control

Most golfers can vastly improve their short shots around the green simply by placing their hands farther down on the club, even to the very bottom of the grip.

Gripping down gives you more control of the club and crisper contact with the ball. It also allows you to stand closer to the ball, keeping your swing path closer to the target line and less around your body (see illustrations), which improves the accuracy of your shots.

Yes

No

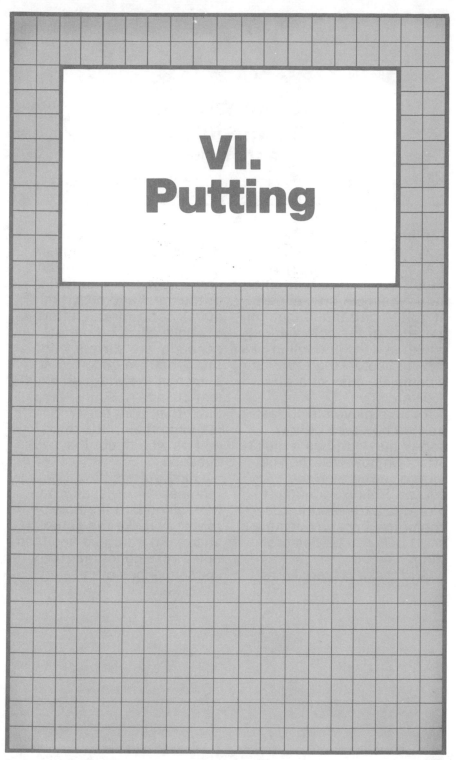

VI.
Putting

Stroke with an "I-can-sink-it" attitude

The finest golfers in the world spend so many hours practicing their putting because they realize that putting is the most crucial part of golf. A putt that hangs on the edge of the hole without falling in adds one full stroke to your score—the same as a complete miss or a 250-yard drive.

The top players also realize that how well or how poorly they putt has a major effect on how well they perform elsewhere on the course. Holing a long putt provides a tremendous psychological boost. Missing a short putt can be demoralizing.

And these players know that consistently excellent putting demands a high degree of mental and physical sensitivity. This fine tuning of the mind and body requires concentrated effort.

Above all, good putters generally are players who *think* they are good putters. They feel they have an excellent chance to sink every putt. They do a better job of planning their putts than golfers who doubt they will succeed.

Good putters have trained themselves to visualize the ball rolling into the hole *before* they make the actual stroke. Poor putters see their putts missing, or fear the consequences of missing.

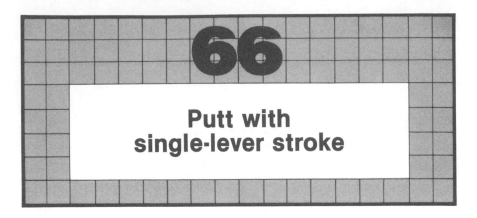

66

Putt with single-lever stroke

The so-called "single-lever" stroke is the simplest in golf because the wrists do not hinge and unhinge. Instead, the relationship between the left arm and the club that you establish before stroking remains constant throughout. Together they form the single lever.

A double-lever action, with the wrists cocking and uncocking, is essential for distance on longer shots, but most good golfers find the single-lever stroke best for putting, where the need for precision is so acute.

When putting, hold the club in your left hand as shown here. Note that the shaft extends upward *between* the thumb pad and heel pad. Primary control of the club should be in the last three fingers of this hand, which will tend to freeze the wrist in its original position.

It will remain in this position during your stroke if you simply swing your left arm back and forward without increasing the pressure in your right hand.

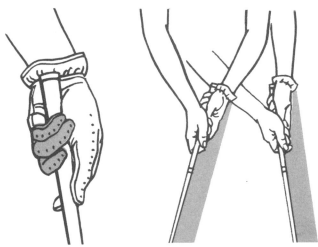

67

Use brand name on ball to 'aim' your putts

You may have noticed how carefully many of the touring professionals replace a ball that has been marked and lifted on the green. In many instances these players are repositioning the ball in a way that will improve their chances of sinking the putt.

They set the ball down so that the lettering on its cover extends directly down the path on which they wish to start the ball rolling.

By simply squaring the putterface to that lettering, they can be better assured that the putter is aimed correctly. Thereafter, they merely try to move the putter "through the ball" in the direction that the lettering extends.

This technique is especially helpful on shorter putts where directional accuracy is extremely vital. On long putts you should use the lettering to help you aim correctly, but thereafter you should "switch off" directional thoughts and focus solely on making the ball roll the correct distance.

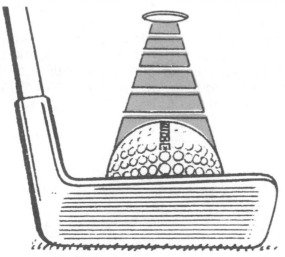

Double-check your putting stance

Inconsistent putting is often the result of inadvertently varying the distance you stand from the ball.

For instance, the right-hander who stands too far from the ball will tend to aim to the right and swing the putter on more or less the same rightward path. Often he will overcorrect for the error by closing the putter-face—turning it to the left—at contact.

Standing too close to the ball tends to cause aiming and stroking to the left, but often with the face open to the right at contact.

To consistently aim and stroke down the correct path with the putterface square, you should always stand just far enough from the ball so that your eyes are set directly over the target line.

To find this position during practice, first address the ball as you normally would, then dangle the club from the bridge of your nose as shown in the illustration. The putterhead will identify the position of your eyes in relation to the ball.

Notice that the club is held lightly at the top of the shaft with the thumb and forefinger. The putterhead runs parallel with the line, not across it. Actually, it should cover the line just behind the ball from your view. Also, note that the player has not changed his posture during the course of lifting the putter into position.

69

Fine-tune your touch with 4-ball drill

The surest way to save strokes on the greens is to improve your sense of "feel" or "touch."

Here is a good way to increase putting sensitivity.

Obtain four balls, preferably new and of the same brand, that are numbered 1, 2, 3 and 4.

Line up these balls on the practice green in numerical order, each the same distance from a hole.

Putt them to the hole in order, trying to make them go in, but do not look up to see where they have actually finished until you have putted all four balls.

As you stroke each ball, sense how far you think it will roll. Decide if it will finish (a) short of the hole or past it and (b) short of any balls you already have stroked or past them.

Finally, check to see where each numbered ball actually finished. See if it wound up where you thought it would, both in relation to the hole and to the other balls.

Repeat the drill until you can make all four balls finish either in or close to the hole. Then repeat the procedure on other putts of different lengths.

This sort of practice will improve your putting almost immediately. You will be amazed at the amount of sensitivity you can develop.

Do not continue this drill at any one practice session once you begin to find that your sense of distance and your ability to concentrate are beginning to wane, as they inevitably will after a while.

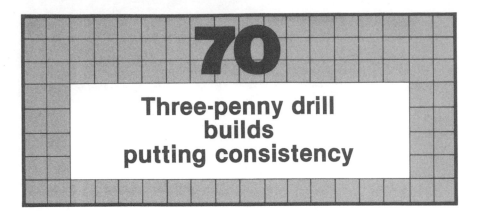

70
Three-penny drill builds putting consistency

Here's a good way to improve your putting in your own home, providing you have fairly smooth, wall-to-wall carpeting in one room.

Position three pennies (or other coins) and your ball as shown. Note that the ball is positioned so the toe end of the putter almost touches the side wall.

(If you lack sufficient wall

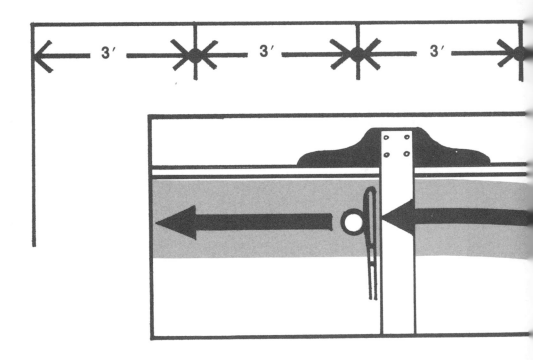

area that is clear of furniture, merely putt in the center of the room. Put two additional clubs on the floor—one alongside your ball and one beyond your farthest target coin—to simulate the side and end walls.)

As you putt:

1. Always align your putterhead at an angle square to the side wall.

2. Swing your arms on a path that *never* lets your putterhead bump the wall.

3. Swing your arms at a pace that will make the putt finish just *beyond* your target coin.

Just 10 or 15 minutes practice every day or two will teach you to aim on target, develop a stroke path that helps assure solid contact and develop a sense of feel for the amount of arm motion needed from different distances.

While your particular carpeting may not be identical to the texture of actual grass, you will find it quite simple to apply the basic *sensitivity for distance* that you develop at home to any putting surface on any course.

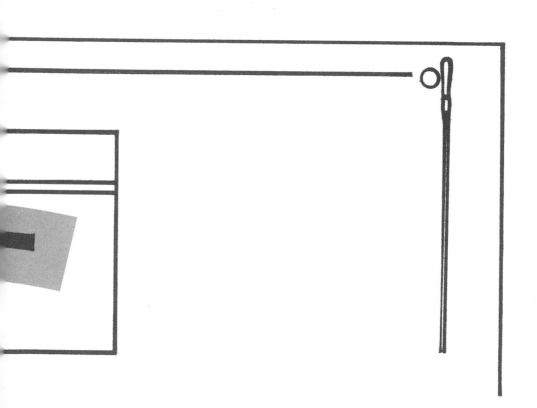

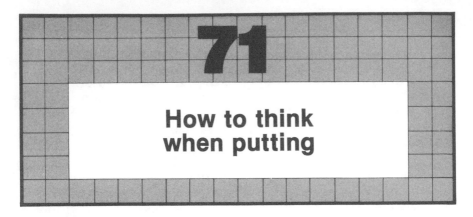

How to think when putting

The golfer who learns to think well when putting will save many strokes on the greens, even though his or her physical technique may lack refinement.

On long putts, once you have determined your intended line and aimed the putter accordingly, it is wise to concentrate solely on making the ball roll the correct distance. More three-putt greens result from the first putt being too long or too short than from being too far off-line.

However, on short putts— those of less than five feet— the problem of three-putting is considerably less. Direction becomes much more important.

On shorter putts, visualize the line you want the ball to take and then aim the putter down that line. Both before and during your stroke, concentrate solely on making your putter move down the line *after* it strikes the ball (see illustration).

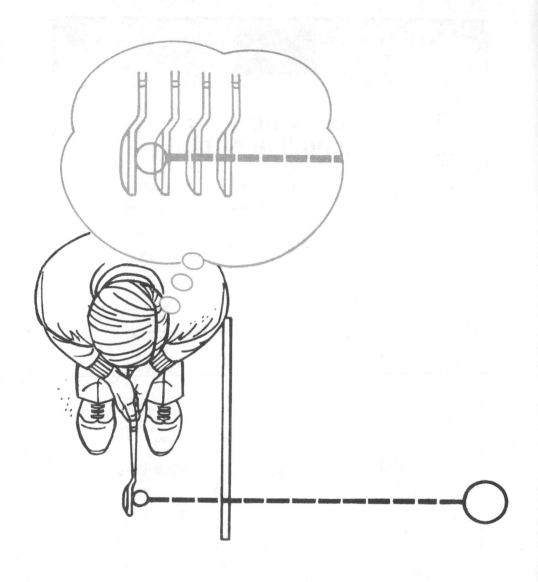

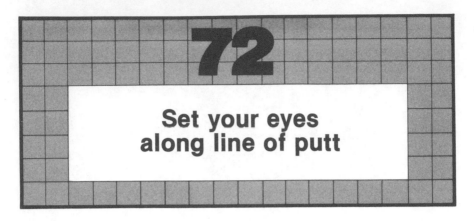

Set your eyes along line of putt

The way you align your eyes before swinging is extremely important on all shots, but especially on putts, where accuracy can save a full shot.

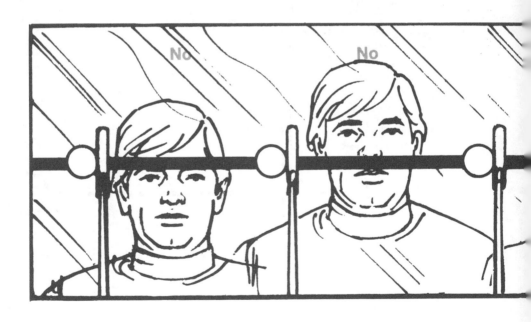

This is true because eye positioning helps determine how you view the upcoming putt, and thus where you will aim and swing the putter.

You should set up to all golf shots with your eyes aligned parallel to your target line. On putts, however, they should also be set directly above this line (see correct and incorrect examples).

A good way to check your eye positioning on putts is to simply lay a mirror on the floor, as shown, with a strip of tape across it indicating the putting line.

With the putter in hand, square its face to that line and position your eyes so that the tape masks their image from your view.

Step into this position a few times until you can sense how you feel when your eyes are properly positioned. Duplicate this feeling when you play. Periodically check your eye position in the mirror whenever your putting starts to falter.

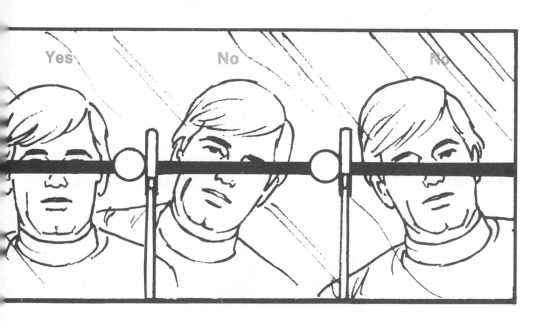

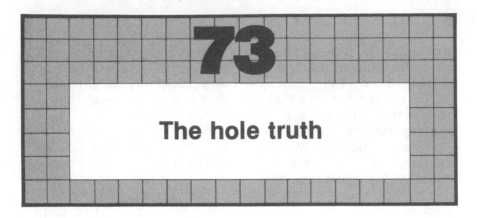

The hole truth

Good putting stems largely from positive thinking. You'll sink more putts if you believe you can.

To this end, golfers should be aware that the hole is more than 2½ times wider than the ball. The margin for error may be bigger than you thought.

Observe the drawing, and bring it to mind the next time you step up to a critical putt.

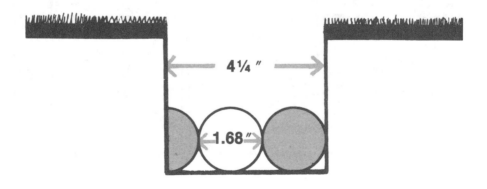

4¼"

1.68"

74

Length of backstroke key to solid contact

One of the best things you can do to become a good putter is simply to strike each putt as solidly as possible. As obvious as this may seem, even experienced players frequently become so engrossed in various aspects of their putting that they lose sight of this goal.

Solid contact on every putt is necessary for developing a keen sense of distance on the greens—inconsistent contact creates putts of inconsistent length.

Your ability to make solid contact depends largely on developing the right amount of backstroke. If your backstroke is too short, you will tend to overaccelerate your forward stroke in order to make the ball go a given distance. If it is too long, you will tend to decelerate into the ball to avoid hitting too far.

When you practice putting, spend some time stroking putts of the same length with varying lengths of backstroke. Find the length that gives you best contact time after time while still rolling the ball the correct distance. Then try to apply that same proportion of backstroke to putts of varying lengths.

If your putting goes sour, once again experiment with a longer and shorter backstroke until you regain solid contact.

Look for an overall tilt to greens

It is second nature for golfers to look for slope between the ball and the hole, and to allow for its influence on the upcoming putt.

But golfers often fail to notice an overall tilt in many greens, which offsets the more apparent slope between the ball and the hole.

Thus, it is wise to develop the habit of looking for steep upslopes or downslopes in the terrain as you walk to the green. More often than not a steep slope near the green causes the green itself to be tilted in the same general direction.

For instance, if there is a steep upslope behind the green or a steep downslope in front of it, the green probably tilts from back to front. A steep incline off to the right, say, or a valley on the left, might well indicate that the green slants from right to left.

To confirm your suspicion that a green is tilted, always look for the effect of such tilt in the putts of others who play before you.

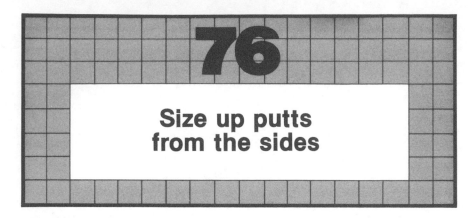

76

Size up putts from the sides

You will sink more putts if you develop the habit of first glancing at them from the sides (see illustration). Do it quickly—and unobtrusively if others are preparing to putt—so as not to waste time.

By viewing a putt from the sides, you will be able to detect sidehill break by noting a difference in the terrain as seen from the two perspectives. From one side the green will appear to be sloping toward you. From the other side it will appear to be level or sloping away from you. If you see no difference between the two views, you at least will know that the putt is straight.

Looking at a putt from the sides also gives you a much better impression of its length than you would get by reading it only from behind the ball. The side views also reveal clearly if the putt will be uphill or downhill.

Once you gain a general impression of the putt by viewing it from the sides, you then should sight it from behind the ball to determine its specific path.

77

How to play sloping putts

There are certain kinds of putts that most golfers consistently misdirect. The problem occurs on uphill and downhill putts when there is also a degree of sidehill slope to consider.

The unfortunate tendency is to allow for too much curve on the uphill putt and for too little on the downhiller.

This happens when the player fails to realize that

- For the uphill putt to reach the hole, the ball must move relatively fast during the early and middle stages of its trip. Because it is rolling fast, the sidehill slope has very little effect on its direction.
- For the downhill putt to stop at the hole, rather than far beyond, it must roll at a relatively slow speed all the way. The slower-moving ball is more susceptible to the effect of any sidehill slope.

In short, allow for less curve than normal on uphill putts; allow for more curve than normal on downhill putts.

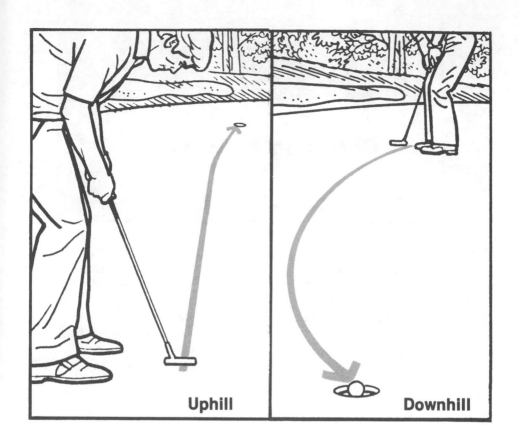

Uphill

Downhill

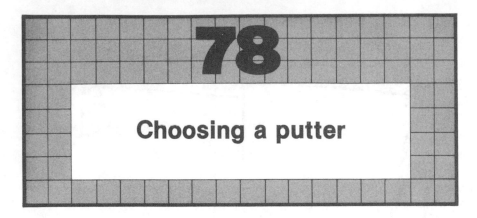

Choosing a putter

Today there is a seemingly endless variety of putters on the market. Here are some suggestions for finding the one that best suits your personal needs:

First, seek a putter that, when soled flat on the ground or a floor, allows you to stand close enough to the clubhead so that your eyes are directly over your putting line. Being forced to stand too far from the line makes it more difficult to aim and stroke down that line.

Putters that are too long tend to force you to stand too far from the line. So do those with a relatively flat "lie," as opposed to those in which the shaft enters the putterhead at an angle closer to vertical.

Second, seek a putter that you find is simple to aim.

Third, look for one that is easy to control.

Finally, look upon the putter you buy as a friend for life. The vast majority of great putters have overcome occasional bad streaks on the greens by working on their technique rather than seeking a new piece of equipment.

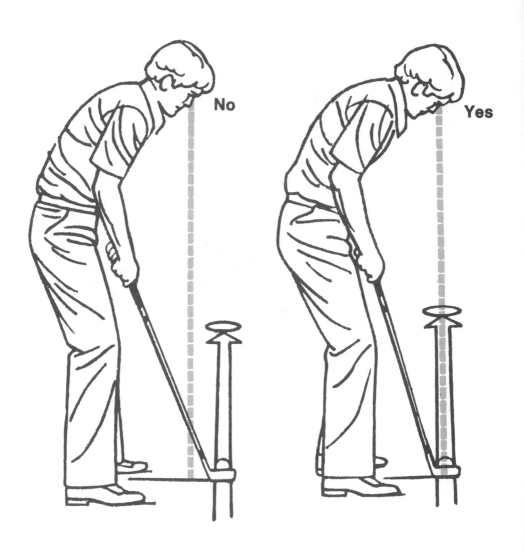

No

Yes

Putting from off the green

Many golfers do not realize that the putter can be used effectively on shots from off the putting surface.

The advantage of putting these shots usually is that solid contact is all but assured. The drawback is that the ball's roll can be adversely affected by the less-manicured area the shot must cover before reaching the green.

Solid contact with the putter requires first that the back side of the ball be well exposed (first drawing). A ball on bare ground is easier to contact with a putter.

Your second consideration is the distance between the ball and the green (second illustration). In close, favor putting, because there is less chance that the ball will be slowed or deflected off-line before reaching the green.

Your third consideration is the length and texture of the grass in the intervening area (third drawing). Smooth, short-cropped grass favors putting. Grass that is long, or pocked with bare areas, or lying toward your ball, almost invariably demands a chip shot that clears this area.

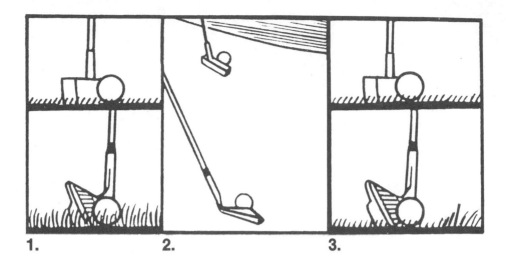

1.　　　　　　2.　　　　　　3.

VII.
Trouble
Shots

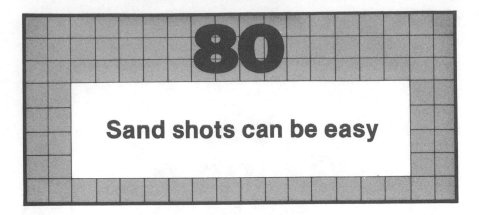

Sand shots can be easy

For years good golfers have been telling poor players that shots from sand are easy. For years poor players have disbelieved it.

Sand shots *are* easy, if you have a sand wedge, a little understanding and some time to practice in a bunker.

Why? Because normal sand shots do not require precise striking.

Look at it this way. To make a solid shot off grass, you must contact the *back* of the ball near the *center* of the clubface. (1) Your margin for error is relatively slight, a fraction of an inch in any direction.

On normal sand shots the clubhead need not, and should not, directly contact the ball at all. It can enter

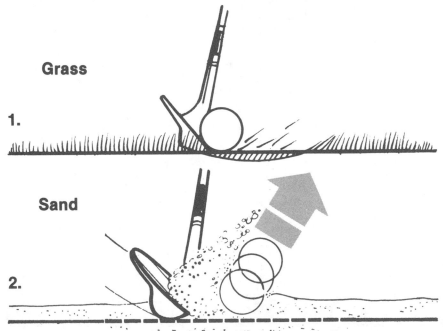

Grass

1.

Sand

2.

the sand anywhere from one to six inches behind the ball. (2) Thereafter it displaces a cushion of sand that propels the ball onto the green. Your margin for error is several inches.

The first step toward successful bunker play is to buy a sand wedge. This club is specially constructed to ride through the sand under the ball without cutting in so deeply that it loses too much momentum.

You should hold the sand club so that it will face somewhat to the right of your target when you position your hands normally. The farther you aim it to the right, the shallower your cut of sand will tend to be.

Next, work your toes downward into the sand. This toeing gives you firm footing for good balance. It also lowers your body slightly in relation to the ball, so that the clubhead will enter the sand behind the ball when you make your normal golf swing.

Aim the clubface to the right of or at your target according to whether you wish to take a shallow or deeper cut of sand (3). Swing sharply upward and then downward through the sand with your arms, and finish your forward swing with a full and aggressive follow-through.

Finally, learn to control the length of your sand shots by regulating the length—not the force—of your swing. Start by finding the length you achieve with a full swing.

With practice, sand shots will become as simple as they are supposed to be.

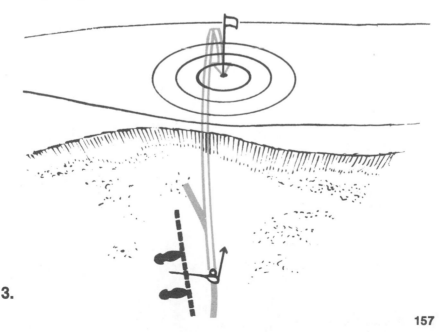

3.

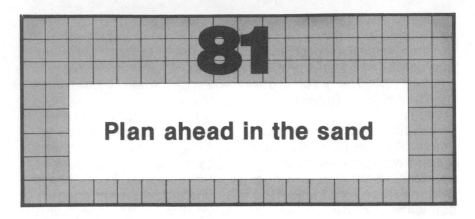

81

Plan ahead in the sand

Whenever you find yourself in a bunker alongside a green, always look beyond the flagstick to see where your shot might finish if it goes too far.

Often you will find that it would be better to play your shot a few feet to one side of the hole rather than right at it. This might allow you to play your next shot from grass, rather than from another bunker.

Or the green might be configured so that playing to the side of the hole gives you more putting surface on which to stop a long bunker shot.

Planning ahead in this manner not only will save you shots; it also will ease your mind so you can make a freer, more confident stroke on the shot at hand.

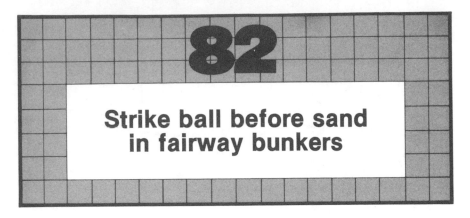

82

Strike ball before sand in fairway bunkers

The long shot from a fairway sand bunker mystifies most golfers. Usually they fail because they do not apply the clubhead to the ball BEFORE it hits the sand (see drawing), unlike a normal sand shot near a green.

Set up to the shot with the ball a bit farther toward your right foot (see drawing). This allows your clubhead to contact the ball a bit earlier than normal, before it reaches sand level.

If you choose to dig your feet into the sand—a good idea to assure a solid footing—you must also choke down on the clubshaft a commensurate amount to avoid scooping the clubhead into the sand behind the ball.

Finally, if there is a hill in front of the bunker that your ball must clear, be sure to use a club with more loft than you normally would choose. You will need the extra loft because playing the ball farther back in your stance will make the shot fly lower than usual.

(This procedure works especially well when the ball is not buried. If it is buried, you will need to take some sand as you strike the ball.)

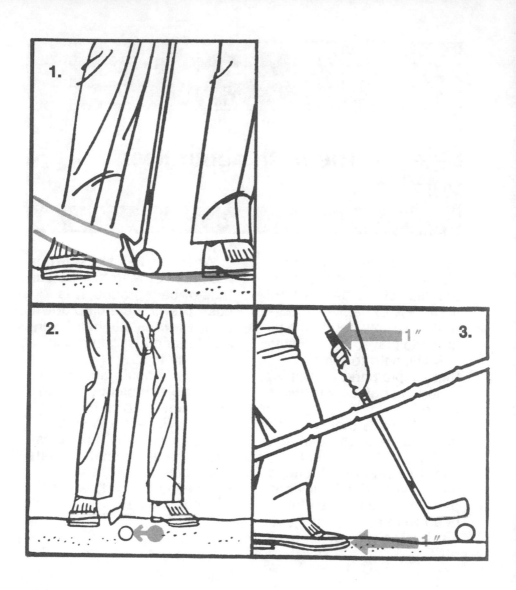

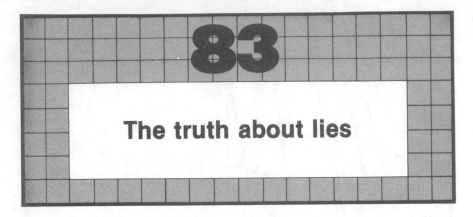

The truth about lies

To make solid contact golfers should appreciate that the "lie" of the ball—where it sits—is extremely important. It largely determines how the player should swing.

It will help to remember this simple phrase: "Ball up, swing up; ball down, swing down."

This means that when the ball sits up, such as atop a tee or a tuft of grass, it is best to swing the clubhead into it on a slightly upward path, much as if the clubhead were an airplane just leaving the runway on take-off.

When the ball sits down in the grass or rests on the surface of bare ground, it is best to swing the club down to it, as if the clubhead were an airplane just coming in for a landing.

When in doubt about the lie being sufficiently up to swing up, or down to swing down, it is best to swing down to the ball. This helps avoid the unfortunate results that occur when the club catches in the turf before it reaches the ball.

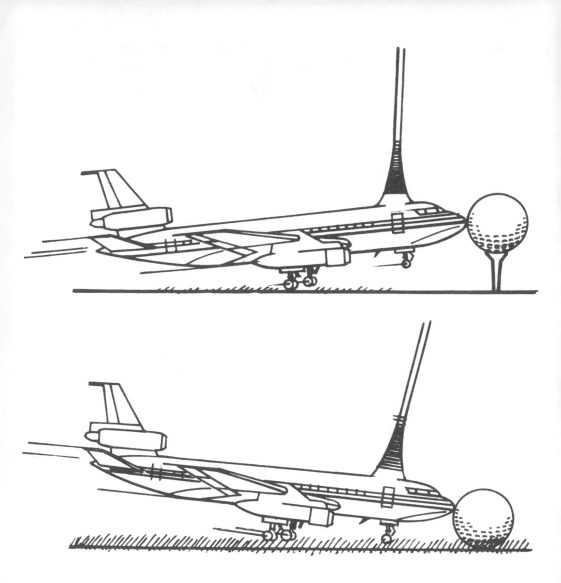

Rehearse swing from all hilly lies

It takes experience to learn to make solid contact on shots from hilly terrain. Even a slight slope can impair your ability to swing in balance. It can also alter the spot where your clubhead returns to the ground.

By making a few practice swings alongside the ball, you can program yourself to retain your balance as you play the shot, perhaps by reducing the amount of effort that you exert.

By also noting just where your clubhead touches down during your rehearsal swings, you can tell whether you will need to stand closer to the ball, or farther from it, or more to the left or right, for the upcoming shot.

85

Overcome grassy lies with club selection

One of your major golfing enemies is the grass immediately behind your ball. It can slow your club's forward movement and prevent solid contact.

Your ability to cope with this enemy depends largely on the weapon you select.

If your ball is nestled down in unusually thick grass—even in the fairway—you should choose an iron club of at least 4-iron loft rather than a wood. Generally, the higher and thicker the grass around your ball,

the higher the number of iron you should choose. The iron's sharper blade will cut through the grass to the ball.

You automatically will swing the iron into the ball on a more downward angle than you would the longer-shafted wood, avoiding some of the grass your clubhead otherwise would encounter.

Also, the iron club will be more lofted than the wood. This makes the ball take off more abruptly upward, avoiding grass in front of the ball.

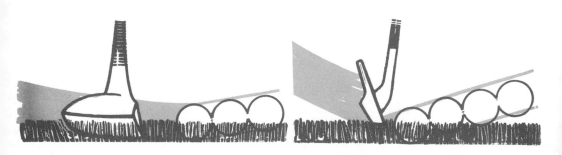

Adjust aim on sidehill lies

If you understand what type of shot to expect from a given type of slope, you can allow for it before you swing. This is particularly important on sidehill lies, because when the ball is above or below your feet, the resultant shot almost always is a curve.

The illustrations show how to compensate for the shots that naturally result from sidehill lies.

When the ball is above your feet (1), the shot will fly to the left. Grip down on the club an inch or two and aim to the right of your target.

When the ball is below your feet (2), the shot will fly to the right. To compensate for this, stand closer to the ball and aim to the left of your target.

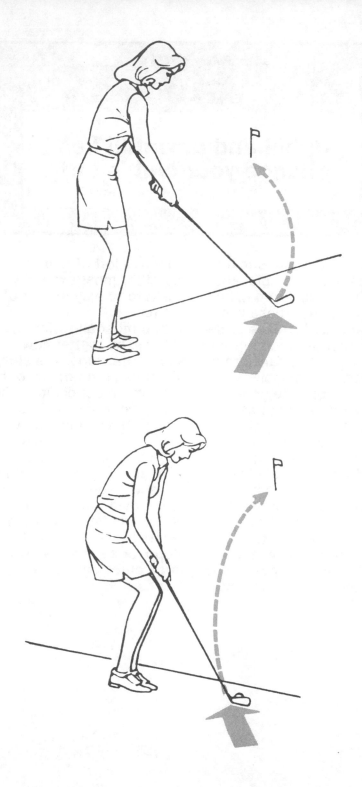

87

Uphill and downhill lies change your club's loft

Many golfers waste strokes because they don't pick the right club to use from uphill or downhill lies. These lies automatically increase or decrease effective club loft and so change the distance to be expected on the shot.

For example, the golfer in the illustration right has recognized the downhill slope and has correctly positioned himself so that the ball is farther back in his stance. However, he has failed to appreciate that the 3-wood he's chosen has in effect become delofted by the change in ball positioning. He is preparing to swing a club that now carries the effective loft of a driver, a club that most *experts* would hesitate to play except off the tee.

You must allow for downhill lies, no matter how subtle the slope. The steeper the slope, the farther to the right you must position the ball in your stance. The farther back you play the ball, the more lofted the club you should choose to achieve normal height and length on the shot. You will need to drop down at least one club—say from a 3-wood to a 4-wood—on a very slight slope, or as much as two or three clubs on steeper slopes.

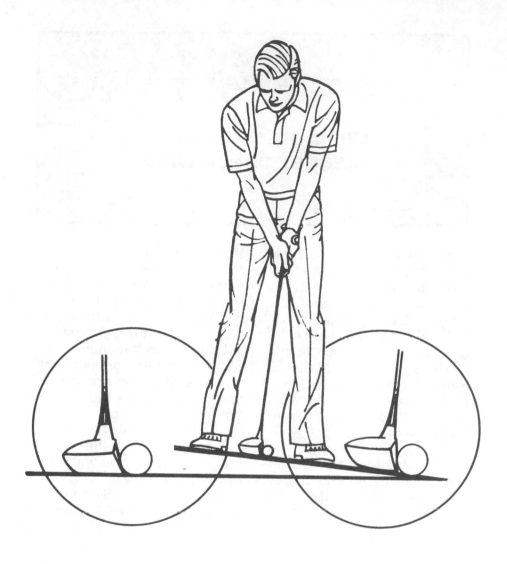

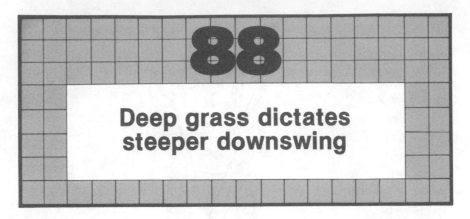

88

Deep grass dictates steeper downswing

When your ball nestles down in the grass, you must adjust. The grass behind the ball will slow down your clubhead, and the grass in front of the ball will slow down the ball during takeoff.

Make your angle of attack more steeply downward, to reduce the amount of grass your clubhead must encounter before impact.

To steepen your angle of attack, play the ball a bit farther back in your stance but keep your hands in their normal position.

Use a more lofted club than usual. The extra loft makes the ball fly out higher and helps it avoid the grass in front of it. Don't be reluctant to use a more lofted club for fear it might cost you length on the shot. Shots from deep grass usually roll farther than normal, and the important thing is to get out of the rough.

The deeper your ball sits down in the grass, the more loft you'll need. You will find that from unusually long or thick grass only a 9-iron or pitching wedge will fly the ball out into safer territory.

89

When to play the ball back

There are several fairly common situations that require playing the ball farther back toward the middle of your stance, rather than opposite the left heel, so that the top end of the club is leading the bottom end both at address and at impact. These situations are

- When the ball rests on bare ground.
- When the grass behind the ball is deeper than normal.
- When the ball sits up well on the sand in a fairway bunker.
- When the ball rests on a downhill slope.

The change of ball position allows the clubhead to make contact while still moving downward, before it reaches the bottom of its arc. Thus the clubhead can safely clear the ground, deep grass, sand or hillside behind the ball.

Because the clubhead is moving more downward at impact, the shot will usually fly lower than normal. Therefore, also choose a club with more loft than you might normally select.

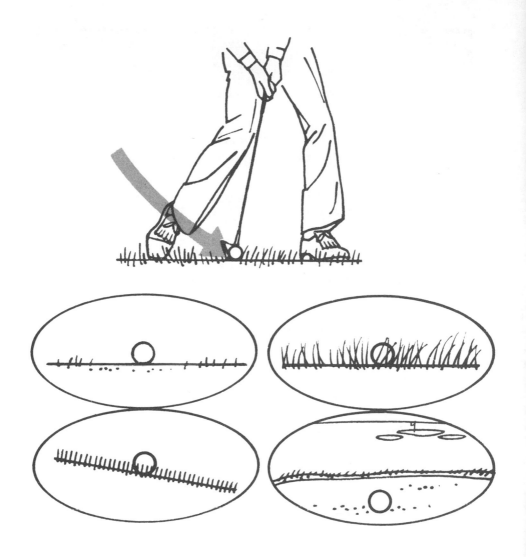

90

Choke down in wet weather

All golfers should be aware that wet grass and turf often produce abnormal shots.

Moist grass tends to lessen friction between the clubface and ball, reducing backspin so the ball flies farther than expected. Soft, wet turf allows the clubhead to penetrate too far into the ground. This extra penetration reduces clubhead speed and shot distance.

One way to minimize both effects is to choke down on the club a half inch or so.

This shortens the effective length of the club and reduces its chances of penetrating too deeply into the turf. It also shortens the length of your swing arc so the ball does not fly quite as far as usual.

Moreover, the more compact swing that results from choking down makes it easier for you to retain your balance while swinging, even though you are standing on a slicker surface.

VIII.
Shot-Saving
Rules

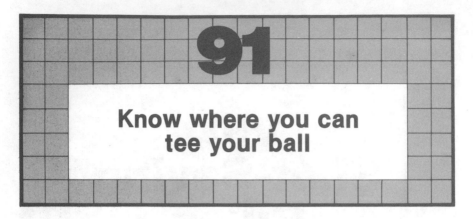

91

Know where you can tee your ball

On each golf hole you are allowed to set your ball atop a wooden or plastic tee for your first shot.

But the rules require that your teed ball sit within the teeing ground. This is a rectangular area two club-lengths in depth, the front and sides defined by the outer limits of two markers (see drawing). You need not stand in this area, however.

If you violate this rule in match play—where the number of holes won determines the winner—your opponent can make you replay your shot, but without penalty.

If you break this rule in stroke play—where total score determines the winner—you must play another tee shot, counting that stroke plus the original and any others made during the interim. If you do not replay your tee shot before starting the next hole, you could be disqualified.

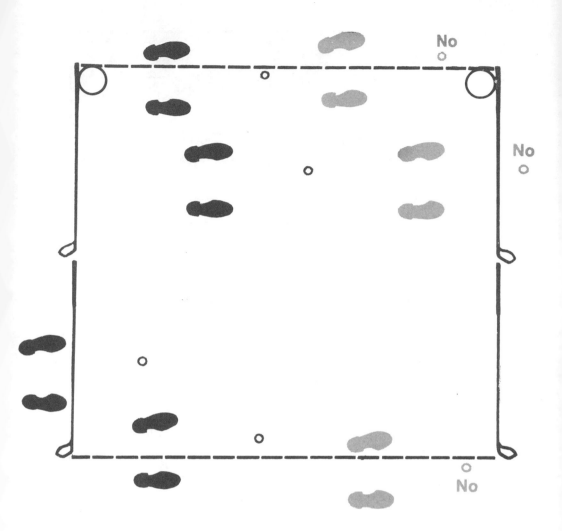

No

No

No

179

Salvage your score from unplayable lies

Be aware that the rules protect you from running up your score trying to play from an impossible situation. They allow you three options when the ball comes to rest in an unplayable lie, such as between two exposed tree roots, against an immovable rock or under a thick bush. (Each option costs one penalty stroke.)

1. You may drop the ball over your shoulder at the spot from where the original shot was struck (Point A in the drawing) and replay from there. You may tee up again and play from within the teeing area if the original shot was from a tee.

2. You may drop a ball within two club-lengths of the unplayable lie, in any direction but not nearer the hole (Point B).

3. You may drop a ball as far behind the unplayable lie as you choose, so long as you keep that position directly between the dropping point and the hole (Line C).

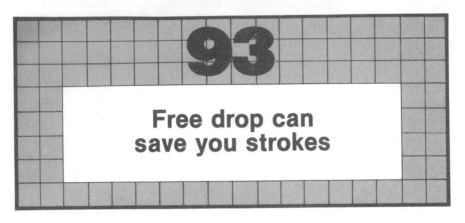

93

Free drop can save you strokes

Golfers should understand the procedure for dropping the ball away from certain problem spots as allowed by the Rules of Golf. You may, for instance, drop your ball without penalty away from ground under repair, a burrowing animal hole, a temporary accumulation of water or an immovable obstruction such as a sprinkler head, ball washer, water fountain or an artificially surfaced road or car path. The free drop is allowed if the problem interferes with your ball, your swing or your stance.

Lift your ball and take it to the nearest point of relief that is not nearer the hole. Stand within one club-length of that spot, face the hole and drop the ball over your shoulder. You must play the ball from where it comes to rest unless

1. It touches you or your clothing before hitting the ground.

2. It rolls more than two club-lengths from where the ball hits the ground.

3. It finishes nearer the hole than its original position.

4. It finishes in a hazard (sand or water) or out-of-bounds.

In any of these four instances, you drop again without penalty. If your drop is unsuccessful on your second try, you may place the ball where it first struck the ground on that attempt.

So long as your drop is valid, it doesn't matter if the ball finishes in a better or worse position than its original one.

If you encounter one of these drop situations on the green, you should place, not drop, your ball at the nearest point of relief not nearer the hole.

In a sand or water hazard, you must drop at the nearest point of relief not nearer the hole in that hazard. To drop away from a hazard calls for a one-stroke penalty.

When ball is moved by accident

Golfers sometimes move the ball accidentally. Here are some rules regarding this occurrence.

If your ball falls off the tee and you don't continue to swing at it, you need not count a stroke. Merely tee it again and start over.

You need not count a stroke if you move your ball accidentally while marking it on the green or while measuring to see which ball is farthest from the hole. Replace it before continuing play.

Otherwise, you must count a stroke if you, your partner, your caddies or your equipment accidentally move your ball after you've made your first shot on a hole. Replace it before continuing play.

If your ball moves after you have taken your stance and soled your club, count one stroke and play from where it finished moving.

A ball is considered to have moved only if it finally comes to rest in another place.

Outside aids disallowed

Golf is a game that stresses self-reliance. Therefore the rules disallow certain types of outside aid, both human and mechanical.

For instance, you are not allowed to make a shot while someone holds an umbrella over your head, or bends back a branch that might otherwise interfere with your stroke, or points with his toe or club, say, to where you should play your putt.

It is illegal to use a range-finder, wind gauge or level during play. If you happen to smoke, do not be tempted to set your pipe, cigar or cigarette on the ground in a position that might provide any sort of guidance.

Hand warmers are legal but only for your hands, not to keep your golf balls resilient.

No

Aiding and advising—
what's allowed

The Rules of Golf draw a fine line between legal and illegal aid and advice.

For instance, let's say your ball is down in a valley from where you cannot see the flagstick. It is legal to ask someone where it is located on the green, and you may have someone hold the flag aloft as you play your shot.

You also may ask someone to stand at the top of the hill to show you the line, but only before you make a shot. And it is illegal to leave a marker, such as your golf bag or car, on that line.

97

Don't tamper with anything "fixed or growing"

A rule frequently violated by golfers is the one which disallows the moving, bending or breaking of anything "fixed or growing" in order to improve the lie of the ball, the line of play or the area of one's swing.

It is against the rules, for instance, to press down the ground behind your ball, either with your foot or your club, except before playing a tee shot. The club may be grounded lightly, which simply means letting it rest be- hind the ball. It also is illegal to bend back or break off branches that might interfere with your swing or your ball's flight, or to have someone do this for you.

You may, however, move, bend or break fixed or growing objects during the course of assuming a fair stance and/or swinging.

The penalty for violating this rule is two strokes in stroke play or loss of the hole in match play.

98

Don't ground club in hazard

Golfers frequently break the rules when they encounter a shot where the ball rests in a bunker filled with sand. In such a situation you may not touch the sand with your club before you swing or even during your backswing.

The penalty for this infraction is severe—two shots added to your score in stroke play and loss of the hole in match play.

99

On putts, flagstick should be removed or tended

When your ball is on the putting green and it is your turn to play, you should always have the flagstick removed beforehand, or you should ask that it be tended and then removed before your ball reaches the hole.

Otherwise, if your ball should strike the flagstick—on a shot played from the green—you will be penalized. In match play you would lose the hole. In stroke play you would be penalized two strokes and required to play your next shot from where the ball finished.

If you are playing a shot from off the putting surface and your ball strikes the flagstick, there is no penalty.

100

Rub of the green

Luck is a significant aspect of golf. It is covered by the phrase "the rub of the green."

Your shot is headed directly toward the flagstick but bounces sideways toward a sand trap—rub of the green. It stops in the sand immediately in front of a large pebble, which the rules prohibit moving—more rub of the green.

From there you mis-hit the shot. It looks to be headed for no man's land beyond the green, but snags in the flag and drops straight into the hole—again, rub of the green.

The point is that golf was never meant to be a completely fair game. Skill does not always produce success, nor does lack of skill necessarily create disaster. The good competitor learns to shrug off bad breaks as part of the game, and to accept good fortune as his just reward.

This sort of attitude leads to better scores through productive concentration on the shot at hand, rather than morbid reflection on earlier misfortune.

101

Be sure it's your ball!

Make it a habit to be sure the ball you are about to play is, in fact, yours. Failure to do so has cost many a player an important victory.

Hitting the wrong ball, except from a sand or water hazard, gives your opponent the hole in individual match play. In team match play it forces you to withdraw from the hole, though your partner(s) may continue to play for your side. In stroke play the penalty is two strokes.

Except when it rests in a hazard, you are allowed to lift your ball to identify it. However, you must identify it in the presence of your opponent in match play or a fellow competitor or scorer in stroke play, and you must replace the ball where it was.

If you hit the wrong ball from a hazard, there is no penalty. The player must go back to the hazard, find his own ball and replay the stroke.